LIGHT *of* ONENESS

*All is Unity
and
Unity is Light.*

LLEWELLYN VAUGHAN-LEE

First published in the United States in 2003 by
The Golden Sufi Center
P.O. Box 428, Inverness, California 94937.

Printed and bound by Thomson-Shore, Inc.

Library of Congress Cataloging-in-Publication Data

Vaughan-Lee, Llewellyn.
    Light of oneness / Llewellyn Vaughan-Lee.
        p. cm.
    Includes bibliographical references (p.) and index.
    ISBN 1-890350-07-9 (alk. paper)
    1. Spiritual life. I. Title

BL624.V3855 2003
297.4'4--dc21   2003051630

CONTENTS

The
lamp
of the
Divine Light
is in the hearts of those
who believe in the
Oneness of God…
By means of the
Divine Light
the heart
becomes
polished
so that it shines like a polished mirror.
When it becomes a mirror one can
see in it the reflection of existing
things and the reflection of the
Kingdom of God
as they really are.

AT-TIRMIDHÎ

PREFACE

Throughout this book, in an effort to maintain continuity and simplicity of text, God, the Great Beloved, is referred to as He. Of course, the Absolute Truth is neither masculine nor feminine. As much as It has a divine masculine side, so It has an awe-inspiring feminine aspect.

$\mathcal{I}$NTRODUCTION

I saw Eternity the other night
Like a great Ring of pure and endless light.

Henry Vaughan[1]

A CONSCIOUSNESS OF ONENESS

We stand at the edge of a new time when so many things
we have never imagined are finally possible. Many of us
sense these new possibilities, but are unsure of what to
do to help them manifest in our lives and in our world.
But part of the evolution of humanity is the unveiling of
knowledge. When we are given the opportunity to take
a step, we are also given the knowledge needed to do so.

A consciousness of oneness, an awareness of the
unity of life, is the next stage in our collective evolution.
The light of oneness, which is now present all around us,
contains the knowledge needed to enter this new time.
In order to be open to this knowledge and emerge within
this consciousness of oneness, we must abandon the
dynamics of duality that have shaped our previous era.

The dynamics of oneness are very different from the
dynamics of duality and separation. That we are separate
from God has been a basic religious imprint. That we are
separate from nature has determined our relationship to
the ecosystem. That we are separate from each other has

been the foundation of our political, legal, and social systems. Dynamics of duality have embedded our world in conflict and patterns of opposition. Can we escape the ritual of conflict? Can we recognize that life does not need to be a battle? Can we afford to continue fighting each other and nature itself? A different archetype is emerging within the collective psyche of humanity, an archetype not defined by the constellation of opposites.

This reorientation towards a living understanding of oneness offers the possibility of a union of inner and outer, of the one and the many. Inner and outer life can become more connected, the individual and the whole more consciously aligned. And energy that has become too focused on the image of individual spiritual progress can be given back to life where it is desperately needed. The world needs our spiritual attention; the whole needs to be nourished from the heart of the mystic. Life is not a problem to be solved. It is a living organic being glorifying God and evolving to survive. Only when we bring together the spiritual and the physical can we fully participate in what is happening within us and our world. And only with our participation can the world itself come alive with a new quality of peace beyond opposition, freedom that is independent of power dynamics, and love that flows where it is needed, sustaining the planet with divine presence.

One of the most pressing needs of the time is to unify the apparent opposites of spirit and matter. This will enable the magic inherent in matter, the spiritual potential of matter, to awaken and help change the world. But this can only happen through a consciousness of oneness. The constellation of opposites that has polarized spirit and matter is more dangerous than the outer battles we have been fighting. It denies life a vital power. Life needs this power, this magic, to evolve. Without it life will remain stagnant; the changes that are happening in the inner world will not be born into life. The physical world will just reflect the wasteland of our material culture.

Access to this magic is held within the consciousness of humanity. But we have forgotten this. Even humanity's role as guardians of the planet we have understood solely on a physical level. We are like parents thinking our child needs only food and clothing, not love, care, or education. The planet is a dancing creation of spirit and matter, spinning on an axis of love. It has energy centers that need to be awakened, places of power that need to be tended with devotion.

Can we leave behind the attitude that sees opposites creating conflict, and instead become open to the potential of opposites to unite? If we can, we will be in tune with what is happening, and can participate in the way spirit and matter come together. The era of the warring brothers is over—its dynamic of winning or losing is past. Now we need to welcome a paradigm in which consciousness does not constellate the opposites but recognizes their deeper union. Only then can the elements that contain this new way of being come into life.

AWAKENING THE HEART OF THE WORLD

At each stage of evolution we are given access to the energy of a higher level. This is how evolution works. We know this in our individual journey: each real stage on the path opens the door to a different level of understanding and a deeper energy. It is the same for the evolution of humanity. As a new energy and level of awareness are given to humanity, the paradigm of the previous era becomes no longer appropriate. This may create insecurity and a reaction to what is new, but that is only a passing stage. What is important is that we welcome the energy that is being given and learn how to work with it. The real danger is that we miss the opportunity that comes with the moment of transition.

At any period of real transition, help is given from the inner world. This is most evident in the time before death, when the individual is given grace to help resolve what has been left unfinished in her inner and outer life. How much we allow ourselves to be helped is always a matter of choice. In our present world predicament the help is present, but because we have turned away for so long from the reality of the inner world, we do not know how to access it. The helpers of humanity have to work hard to open up energy fields within human consciousness and the planet so that this help can flow where it is needed. They have to work around the patterns of collective resistance because there is not the time to confront these patterns.

The grace that is being given at this time is not interested in personal development. It is not concerned with individual well-being. Its purpose is to open up the energy channels that exist within our collective psyche and collective consciousness and help the heart of the world awaken. We have become so focused on ourselves we have forgotten what has always been true, that the world itself has a higher nature, and that we are part of this greater reality. This truth was expressed long ago in the *Upanishads*:

> That which is the finest essence—this whole world has that as its soul. That is Reality. That is the Self.[2]

When someone is dying, the gates of grace are open. When the person has entered the next stage of her journey, other help is given, but the opportunities given before death no longer exist. The same is true of the present time of global transition. If a certain work is done now, it will affect the whole cycle of the next era. This is why the need of the present time is so pressing. The energy has an urgency because it can only work within a particular time-frame. This is something that is not generally understood. If this work is not done within the next few years, it will be left undone. The transition into the next age will happen at a lower level.

We need to know that the help is there and we need to learn how to work with it. A new energy of oneness, a new quality of love, is already present in everyday life. But this is only the beginning. Other qualities are being made accessible and they can be directly attuned to the collective. One of these qualities is the peace that belongs to the soul, a peace that is not born from the resolution of conflict because it does not belong to the opposites. This is a peace that is not threatened by the dynamic interplay of the opposites or by change. It can bring harmony and understanding, while it also allows for the misunderstanding and discord that belong to our human experience. It is a peace that belongs to God, to our own divine nature. It is given, and not imposed by force.

How do we help bring these qualities to life? We have forgotten that the human being is a microcosm of the whole, that all levels of reality interpenetrate within our heart, which is not separate from the heart of the world. Just as our hearts can awaken and come to know our divine nature, so too can the heart of the world awaken and come to know its own belonging to God. We only have to turn our own hearts towards what is real and live in the world within this understanding. A heart aligned with love, immersed in oneness, will affect life around it more than we can know.

SPIRITUAL WORK

Spiritual work takes many different forms. Inner purification is an important preliminary work, which involves changing patterns of our behavior and freeing ourself from attitudes and responses that interfere with our aspirations. Psychological inner work is part of this process—confronting the "shadow," the repressed, rejected and unacknowledged parts of our psyche; accepting our wounds; and transforming psychological dynamics and patterns of conditioning. Only when we have gained a degree of inner harmony and emptiness can we hear the voice of our higher Self, and learn to discriminate between inner guidance and the desires of the ego.

Through spiritual work we also develop the qualities we need for the path, for example self-discipline, compassion, patience, perseverance. Through working on our spiritual practices such as meditation and remembrance, we learn to still the mind and be attentive to the needs of the divine in our inner and outer life. We also learn to master our negative qualities, such as anger, greed, jealousy, and judgment. Through this work we are better able to align ourself with our higher nature, and live its qualities in our daily life. We bring our selflessness, awareness, loving-kindness, discrimination and other qualities into our family and workplace, transforming both ourself and our environment. To live according to our higher principles in the midst of the outer world with its distractions and demands is a full-time work.

The spiritual wayfarer gives herself to her inner work and outer service. The Sufis are known as "slaves of the One and servants of the many." We make our contributions to outer life in whatever way we are called, whether through simple acts of loving-kindness or more defined service, helping those in need. We help those in our spiritual community and in daily life. We learn to be always attentive to the needs of our Beloved in whatever form He appears.

There is also another dimension of spiritual work that until now has been mainly hidden, known only to initiates. This is the work done by individuals and spiritual groups on the inner planes, helping humanity from within. Just as the human being is surrounded by an aura of light and energy, so too is the world surrounded by a structure of light. The balance of energy in this structure helps maintain life on the planet. Mystics have always worked with this web of light, for example by reflecting light where there is too much darkness, or holding a space of conscious remembrance, which allows grace to flow into the world.

In the aftermath of the September 11th terrorist attacks this work was almost tangible, as individuals and groups all over the world meditated and prayed, helping to repair the inner fabric of life that was torn apart by the violence of the tragedy. One could feel the cocoon of love and devotion that was being created by all of the souls engaged in this work.

Spiritual groups and individuals have always worked in the inner realms, bringing love and light where they are needed. Through their prayers, devotions, and other practices they work either knowingly or unknowingly. Traditionally His lovers and the *awliyâ*, the friends of God, look after the well-being of the world, "keeping watch on the world and for the world." Much spiritual work happens on the level of the soul where it is veiled from the everyday consciousness even of those who are involved. It is difficult for the mind to comprehend levels of reality beyond its immediate perception, and often it is best for the ego not to know what we are doing. Inflation is a constant danger in this work.

However, there is now a need for wayfarers to know a little of the work that is happening in the inner planes. In the West we have identified spiritual work too much with our individual inner journey or outer acts of service. We need to know that we are a part of a network of mystics who are helping the world come alive with love, working from within to redeem a world that has become desecrated with materialism and forgetfulness.

During the last decade a web made of the lights of the lovers of God began to form around the world. When I first glimpsed this I was awed by its beauty and purpose. I wrote:

> The spinning hearts of the lovers of God are forming the map made of points of light…. At this time His lovers are being positioned around the planet. Some have already been positioned. Some are moving to physical locations while others are having their hearts awakened to this hidden purpose. Slowly this map is being unfolded, and in certain important places lovers are forming clusters of points of light. Certain spiritual groups have been formed or are being formed to contain these clusters as dynamic centers of light.

When this map of light around the world is fully unfolded it will be able to contain and transform the energy structure of the planet. It has the potential to be the bond that will enable the world soul, the *anima mundi*, to be impregnated with a higher consciousness. The hearts of His lovers form part of the hidden heart of the world. As this map is unfolding, so their spinning hearts can open the heart of the world. At this moment in cosmic time the planet is being aligned with its inner source, allowing the world to be infused with a certain cosmic energy that can dramatically speed up the evolution of this planet. If the heart of the world opens, it can receive this frequency of cosmic energy and directly implant it into the hearts of people. This would alter human life more than we could imagine. It is to help in this opening of the heart that many old souls have incarnated at this particular time and are working together.[3]

Over the years this web of light and love has become more defined, more interwoven, and has covered more of the planet. For any real and lasting spiritual transformation or awakening to take place, an inner container first needs to be created. This web of light is the inner container for the consciousness of the future, a consciousness of oneness that is being given to humanity.[4] The container for this awakening has been created, but the dynamic energy of oneness needs to be brought into the collective. The web of light needs to be brought down to earth, enfolded into the physical structure of the planet. Women have a specific role to play in this work, as their bodies contain a creative force that unites matter and spirit. This creative principle naturally allows the inner to flow to the outer, nourishing what has been forgotten with the light and love of the divine.

Light of Oneness describes a little of how mystics work in the inner world, using the light of oneness to transform the old patterns and bring a new awareness into the collective. It is a description of an inner landscape that may seem unfamiliar, but is real. This is not a textbook of how to access oneness or work on the inner planes. We are always guided from within in this work; the knowledge is given from heart to heart, from soul to soul. But it may be helpful to know that this work is taking place, that a new awareness is being made accessible that can transform life beyond our imaginings. It can open a doorway to a different horizon, expand our understanding of spiritual work and the potential for global transformation, and thus enable us to participate in ways that until now have been unknown.

Central to our present time of transition is a need to become more conscious, to learn to participate knowingly. Much knowledge that until now has been kept hidden is being revealed by many different spiritual traditions. This book is about the work of the lovers of God, those who have given themselves in service to their Beloved, and are here to help the awakening of His world.

$\mathscr{L}$IGHT of $\mathscr{O}$NENESS

In the golden city of the heart dwells
The Lord of Love, without parts, without stain.
Know Him as the radiant light of lights.

There shines not the sun, neither moon nor star
Nor flash of lightning nor fire lit on earth.
The Lord is the light reflected by all.
He shining, everything shines after Him.

Mandaka Upanishad[1]

REFLECTING THE LIGHT OF ONENESS

In the depths of nonbeing there is a light, and this light contains the consciousness of the whole of humanity. This light continually flows into life, determining the development of our consciousness and the patterns of our evolution, giving meaning to each moment in time.

This light is part of the essential core of our being. It belongs to all life; it is the awareness of the whole within every particle of existence. Through its effects, all the threads of creation are interwoven into the dynamic spinning organism that is our world.

We can not know this light directly, but we can work with it through an awareness of oneness, a deepening understanding of the interrelatedness of all life. As this light enters the planes of being, it can reveal the mysteries of creation and our responsibilities within the destiny of the whole. It can sweeten the world with the fragrance of divine love, and awaken us within the oneness that is the mystical secret of our relationship to God. It can nourish the world with real freedom and peace, and can help restore balance where dynamics of power and greed have taken control.

Certain individuals are being trained to work with this light, to help give humanity access to the consciousness of the whole. Through the participation of consciousness, this light is guided where it is needed most, unveiling the unity and love in the heart of the world. This work is done through a process of reflection, as the light of the whole is reflected from the higher planes into the midst of life. An individual can be trained to work as a mirror, directing the reflection of light to where it is needed. Through conscious attention and inner alignment, the individual can fine-tune the reflection of light, so that it is focused and filtered, its amount and direction precisely measured.

Normally, this light is filtered from nonbeing to being through all planes of creation. As it permeates each level of creation, it becomes more distorted, less finely attuned. We experience this in our own awareness, as the direct perception of the Self becomes the fragmented perception of the ego. The nature of the ego makes it difficult to see the whole, to step outside of the narrow confines of self-interest. The wider meaning and purpose of the Self are lost in the desires of the ego and its patterns of conditioning.

Through spiritual training and inner work we polish the mirror of the heart—we learn to stay true to the oneness that is our essential nature even as life reflects back to us the unrelenting needs of the ego with its continual desires and its dynamics of projection. Polishing the mirror of the heart is the work of the wayfarer until the eye of the heart begins to open. Then, rather than a fragmented reflection of herself, the wayfarer begins to see with the light that belongs to wholeness, to the unity that is her real nature. This is the light of Truth, the secret substance that is hidden within the heart. In the words of al-Gîlânî:

> Dear friend, your heart is a polished mirror. You must wipe it clean of the veil of dust which has gathered upon it, because it is destined to reflect the light of divine secrets.... It is not the stars that guide us but the divine light.[2]

When the heart of the seeker has been awakened, this natural state of being remains constant. Many way-farers have reached this state of awareness. It can be experienced in different ways—resting in inner peace or love, abiding in God, direct perception, an awareness of unity, or living from the higher Self. In the Sufi tradition it is experienced as the state of becoming "the eyes and ears of God":

> My servant ceases not to draw nigh unto Me by works of devotion, until I love him, and when I love him I am the eye by which he sees and the ear by which he hears.

When the ego has relinquished its hold and we be-come aware of a reality beyond its fragmented vision, we can play a part in life's larger dimension. Immersed in a consciousness of oneness, we are able to participate in the process of His light being reflected into the world.

In Sufism, this work happens through love. Love belongs to oneness; an awakened heart is an open door-way between all levels of existence. The heart of the *sheikh* is merged into his *sheikh*, who is merged into the oneness of God. In the chain of love that belongs to the Sufi path, the *sheikh* reflects light from his heart into the heart of the disciple, through whom the light is reflected into the world. This is a part of the Sufi esoteric tradition.

The *sheikh* is one who has passed from existence to nonexistence, who has been made empty by the imprint of Truth. Although his outer form exists in the reality of this world, his inner nature has been annihilated of all except the indefinable substance of the Beloved. The nonexistence of the *sheikh* enables him to reflect the pure light of love into the heart of his disciple and then into the world. Imagine a lamp that shines through a pinhole onto a polished mirror. The lamp is the light of Truth, the pinhole is the *sheikh*, and the mirror is the heart of the disciple. Just as the positioning of the pinhole can direct the beam of light, so can the essential emptiness of the *sheikh* direct the light towards the mirror of the disciple's heart. The direction of the beam of light and the way the mirror reflects the light determine where the reflected beam will fall. In this way, the *sheikh* and the disciple work together, determining not just where the light will fall, but also the amount and even quality of light that is needed. The more closely the *sheikh* and the disciple work together, the more accurately the light can flow.

Some level of distortion will always exist in this reflection of light, because in this world nothing is perfect. In fact a small degree of distortion is necessary to bring light and love into manifestation. Without distortion the energy would not be accessible; it would be too fine, too pure to be assimilated. However, if there is too much distortion, if the heart is not pure enough, then the disciple will be unable to reflect it, and the light can be damaging. Instead of being reflected out into the world, this powerful light can become caught in the ego structure and psyche of the disciple, where it can unbalance her. It is important that the light be reflected outward, and not get caught in the ego.

It is the responsibility of the *sheikh* to know when the disciple is ready. He needs to be able to measure the degree of distortion that is acceptable and necessary, and to give each disciple the amount of love that is appropriate. Then he can direct his disciples' hearts where the light is needed.

RECLAIMING OUR RELATIONSHIP TO LIFE

The energy of oneness continually flows through life in a fluid organic system. We have the opportunity to reclaim a relationship with life that includes an awareness of this wholeness and allows us to participate responsibly within life as part of its greater unfolding. We can take this step by becoming more conscious of the energy of oneness, of how it connects all life and how it reveals the hidden meaning of each moment. This awareness can help unblock obstructions in the flow of energy through life and help life reflect our inner knowing of divine unity.

The energy patterns of life are very complex, and have been woven together over the centuries. Their structures function not only in the outer world but also *within* the consciousness of humanity. The relationship between consciousness and our interaction with life has been long known by Buddhist and other practitioners. A subtle web of energy flows between our mind and the outer world, constellating the dynamics of our life. Our consciousness and our outer life are part of the same one-ness. Particle physics has begun to probe the interaction between matter and mind, but mystics have understood this interaction for centuries.

The consciousness of oneness is powerful; it needs to be directed into life with care and precision. Like a complicated knot, our collective patterns of isolation need to be carefully untied. Then the energy of life that knows its source can flow more freely, no longer caught in the dynamics of our ego-centered view of the world.

The first step is to disentangle life's energy from our thought-forms of separation. As long as we remain within a mind-set of separation, we cannot understand the way our consciousness interacts with the outer world, how it creates the patterns of *maya* that we regard as our life. We will remain isolated, unaware of the deep potentials of our interdependence with each other and the whole.

The development of consciousness has given us the sense of a separate self, but the next stage of this devel-opment is to realize the greater oneness of which our individual self is an expression. This does not mean a return to unconsciousness, in the way an individual loses herself in a crowd or the collective. Instead it means a celebration of our uniqueness as a part of a whole, as one note in the symphony of life. Only when we take this step towards unity will we be able to see how our indi-vidual self affects and interacts with the whole.

However, powerful energy structures are blocking this step in the development of consciousness. These are hierarchical power structures driven by self-interest. They dominate the way energy flows throughout the world, and are so pervasive that they also have a strong influence on our individual consciousness and attitude.

Sadly, many spiritual groups have also developed organizations based upon hierarchical power structures, not realizing that the very structures they have created limit their potential for real change. The energy patterns of these organizations follow the same lines that give power to a select few, rather than to the whole. Although we may prefer to have leaders who decide what is best for us, these masculine, authoritarian models only too easily promote self-interest and continue to constellate the patterns of power that inhibit real change.

Some spiritual groups have also developed a way of living that rejects the materialistic, power-driven values of our culture. Although it may be valuable to move away from the values of consumerism and greed that dominate so much of our Western collective, the danger of an alternative life-style is that it reconstellates the pattern of duality in a different way. How can one embrace oneness from an attitude of duality? Either we are all a part of the wholeness of life, or we are creating another image of separation. We need to be free of limiting concepts while working within the collective. This is what is meant by the Sufi saying, "Outwardly to be with the people, inwardly to be with God."

Mystics do not seek to overthrow the present system, or impose any new world-order. Their work is far more subtle and subversive. Working on the inner planes, behind the scenes of life, they can free some of the energy patterns that nourish the world. One of the most pervasive problems is our collective forgetfulness of the fact that the world belongs to God. This collective attitude creates an inner barrier against His grace, which can change life far more effectively than can our efforts. Through infusing certain nodes of power with the energy of divine remembrance, mystics can create an inner connection that allows His grace to flow where it is needed.

Together, the *sheikh* and his disciples do this work. The *sheikh's* fundamental nonexistence allows him to exist on all levels of reality. In order to work with the energy of oneness, he is immersed in oneness—beyond time and space—so that he can see the world as a whole, see how its energy structure and patterns of power are formed. This work can only be done from the perspective of the whole; otherwise an imbalance of energy can easily occur.

Working from the depths of nonbeing, immersed in oneness, the *sheikh* can reflect the consciousness of the whole where it is needed. This divine consciousness is very potent, but needs the hearts of individuals in order to be brought into life. One friend had a simple dream that described this work:

> I—or we—have to watch over something that contains the essence of God. There is much ordinary life going on and we are involved in it, but I only dimly remember because I have to concentrate so much on this "something" in order not to lose the link, the focus. The task we have been given is very important, but very, very difficult, almost impossible to perform. This "something" has a form, but not a form in a proper sense. It is an ever-changing container. I can see it and at the same time it can't really be seen. It is very difficult to grasp. What I clearly remember is the knowledge that this "something" contains the substance of God, the task given, and the immense effort necessary in order to try not to lose the focus.

The container in the dream is a special substance of life that can hold the divine consciousness of oneness as it is reflected from the higher planes. This consciousness of oneness includes the essence of the divine, His light, and His love for us. Through this container the light and love of God can flow freely in life. This container is an unconditioned, organic, ever-changing part of life that can respond to the need of the time. The work of the mystic is to keep inner attention while this container is being created, and while the light of oneness flows back into the world. Through focus and attentiveness she lives her inner connection, not as a spiritual idea but as a part of simple ordinary life.

THE SPINNING HEARTS OF THE LOVERS OF GOD

When the energy of divine love is flowing freely into the world, it has the potential to spin. It has long been an esoteric secret that the spinning hearts of the lovers of God keep the world in balance. They form an inner core of love and remembrance without which the world would lose its connection to the source and become unbalanced.

Any time of transition carries the potential for danger, as the old forms do not carry the new energy that is being given. For example, the way that spiritual communities kept separate from worldly life belongs to a time of dualism that is now past.[3] The spinning hearts of the lovers of God are needed in the center of life, in the midst of worldly activities. This is where the energy of divine remembrance is most necessary. It is where the imbalance of power is most precarious. And because this is the center of worldly power, it is also the place of most potential. If enough individual hearts spin with the frequency of divine love, the collective consciousness of the world can start to spin. Then humanity can awaken from its present self-destructive patterns.

This work needs to happen gradually, carefully. Any imbalance could have destructive results. But the masters of love have been working with the flow of energy in the world for centuries. These friends of God have always been with us, most often hidden, living simple lives in the world. Previously their work was most often done from outside of the collective, where the pressures of collective thought-forms had little influence. But they are now being asked to work in the very midst of the collective, because this is where the power and the danger are most present.

The work of these masters is to align their disciples with the energy structure of the world, so that they are working within its energy flow. Then when their hearts are opened they can receive and reflect the light of divine oneness directly into the collective. This energy, which contains within it a knowing that everything belongs to God, is given according to the receptive ability of the disciple and the need of the environment— the place in the world where the disciple is present. From heart to heart, from soul to soul, the energy is given, and then from the disciple it flows out into the world, into the places where this most precious substance is required.

Many wayfarers are familiar with the experience of their hearts' being used to touch the hearts of others. Often this work is done without their knowledge, but there are also instances when, in the company of another person, one might feel a sudden softness or warmth within the heart, as love flows from heart to heart. This transmission of love is part of the way His lovers have always worked in the world.

What is different at this time is that the hearts of mystics are being used to directly infuse the collective with divine consciousness. Collective consciousness is a dense cloud of values, thought-forms, and energy patterns that influence people more than they know. But the light of oneness has tremendous power and can break up the density of the collective, allowing what is free and real to flow into the consciousness of the whole.

This is the work of mystics, and at the present time much of this work needs to be done in the midst of life. We are no longer focused on individual progress, but in helping the evolution of the whole. This is the next turning in our spiritual evolution, the next step in God's revelation of Himself within His world.

NEW ENERGY CENTERS IN THE COLLECTIVE

The spinning hearts of His lovers are being used to reflect divine love and light directly into collective consciousness. But there is also another work being done that includes awakening new energy centers in the midst of life. Centers of power exist within the collective—what Carl Jung called archetypal forces, the gods of the ancient world. The way different centers are awakened, the shift and flow of these qualities of energy, are the determining factors of much of human history. Jung knew their significance when he wrote, "The archetypes are the great decisive forces, they bring about the real events."[4]

The masters of love have always known the existence of these energy centers, their meaning and purpose. They are trained to work with these forces, to keep them balanced and help their energy flow in a way that can benefit humanity. Different energy centers have different purposes, affecting life in different ways. Some energy centers belong to our spiritual beliefs, while others inform our understanding of science, our development of technology. Others express themselves through our patterns of human relationships—the power of the ideal of romantic love in the West, for example, is a direct expression of an archetypal energy. Some energy centers are more active at different periods in history. Some energy centers become active in times of war, while others express themselves in cultural movements, as for example in the awakening that occurred in the Renaissance in Europe.

There are also centers of power that are dormant. Some of these centers have not been awakened for millennia. Others have never been activated. They belong to different eras of human development, as different influxes of energy are needed at different times in our history. They give us the opportunity for change and evolution. There is a way to activate and open these dormant centers so that their energy gradually flows into the collective without causing too much disturbance.

The energy centers that need to be activated at the present time are most accessible from within the collective. They are hidden and yet completely visible. This is a part of their protection. They are nothing special and thus easily overlooked. Even most spiritual practitioners would not notice them because they do not reflect any of the values we associate with spiritual development. For example, many seekers still look for the security of some defined spiritual structure, not knowing that these doors are shut, that it is now the fluid, organic interrelationship between our inner and outer life that reveals His oneness.

These new centers of energy belong to a totally different vibration of consciousness, and they cannot be seen with the eyes of self-interest, either worldly or spiritual. Yet these centers are totally present in the midst of life, waiting, needing to be awakened. And the collective is hungry for the new life that can only begin to flow when this energy is present.

The work of activating these centers of energy is being done through love and through the spinning hearts of the lovers of God.

𝒜WAKENING the 𝒲ORLD

You've traveled up ten thousand steps in search of the Dharma.
So many long days in the archives, copying, copying.
The gravity of the Tang and the profundity of the Sung
make heavy baggage.
Here! I've picked you a bunch of wildflowers.
Their meaning is the same
but they're much easier to carry.

Hsu Yun[1]

THE SECRET SUBSTANCE OF CREATION

Creation contains a substance that enables oneness to reveal itself through the multiplicity of life. This substance is part of the mystery of manifestation, the secret of God's revelation on earth. It is the world's remembrance, its praise and prayer. Without it, there can be no awareness of God's presence in the world, no awareness of the one within the many. This substance is hinted at in the Sufi saying, "the secret of the word *Kun!* [Be]."

This substance exists within all creation, and like all aspects of life it has the potential to transform and evolve. As it transforms, the divine oneness in life becomes more evident. This is where we stand in the evolution of the consciousness of the world—at a point of new awakening, at which all of life can realize a more conscious relationship with the divine.

Consciousness depends upon the process of reflection. Without reflection, there is no knowing. Just as light's reflection off matter allows us to see shapes and forms, so too does awareness of oneness in life depend on the reflection of light off this substance in creation. This secret substance allows the light of oneness to be reflected into the world, revealing His presence in the multiplicity of existence.

The collective is now being given a basic awareness of life's oneness. From ecologists to global corporations to internet users, we all are becoming more aware of the interconnectedness of life, of how the individual interacts with the whole. Corporations now understand that the marketplace extends farther than it ever has, and their success depends upon taking into account this more inclusive perspective. Ecologists and economists both know that subtle changes in one part of the world affect the rest of the world. And with a few strokes on a keyboard we can access information from almost anywhere. Time and space are less restrictive than ever—events from across the globe can be instantly present in our consciousness.

Just as the collective is being given an increased understanding of how oneness works in the world, so too are spiritual seekers being given greater awareness of the deeper reality of divine oneness—that all the world belongs to God, that creation sings the song of its Creator. This belonging is held deep in the unconscious of the world, but in human beings it can become conscious; we can know that all life looks to the Creator. And this knowledge can help nourish the world, awakening the world to its own divine nature.

Spiritual practices can be a way of accessing the secret substance of creation, and transforming it so that it can be used in the evolution of the whole. For example, in Mahayana Buddhism, one is often instructed to generate compassion before beginning any practice. This activates the wisdom of oneness within the heart, orienting the practitioner in the appropriate relationship of service to the world and linking his own transformation to the transformation of all beings.

Practices that work with the breath also give us access to the substance of our own transformation and link us within the matrix of life, thereby allowing our consciousness to affect life itself. With each breath we take, we breathe in the energy of life. Sufis repeat the *dhikr*, combining the breath with the name of God, and so infuse His invisible presence into the flow of the energy of life. By repeating the *dhikr*, Sufis consciously acknowledge the Beloved as the root of our existence and the agent of our transformation. Repeating His name with each breath, we acknowledge that all life belongs to Him. This conscious acknowledgment has tremendous power.

Traditionally, the process of spiritual awakening has primarily depended on individuals focusing on their own practice. But now there is the possibility of infusing spiritual consciousness into the world as a whole. This would enable the world to remember its real nature. At the present time the world is still asleep, locked in forgetfulness. If the world were to awaken, the change in the quality of all life would be immense, unimaginable.

The container has been created for this work. A flowing organic structure of light and love has been formed around the world. This structure is linked to the oneness of life through the hearts of those who love God and all those committed to the work of awakening the world. But this work cannot be done solely on the inner planes through meditation or other practices. Every level of life needs to be infused with the energy of remembrance. This means we need to direct our spiritual consciousness into the midst of life. Then the sacred substance within creation can begin to spin with the frequency of divine awareness. Once it starts to spin at a certain frequency, it activates an organic chemistry within life that will change life as we know it.

Because we have been conditioned to see life and the world from a purely physical perspective, we do not even notice that the world is asleep. We see life through the eyes of our conditioning, unaware of what is waiting to happen. But the mystic knows the world as a reflection of That which she loves; from a perspective of love she knows there is no separation between the infinite and the finite.

The substance of spiritual transformation is in the very cellular structure of life. It has to do with the way energy forms into matter. The transformation of energy into matter is one of the mysteries of creation. It is a continual process in which the invisible comes into form. Particle physics has shown us that the world of matter is not as it appears, but is a constantly changing dance of probability. Energy and matter are different images of the same reality. But there is a dynamic of transition when energy takes on form. This is part of the wonder of revelation, the instant in which His invisible presence becomes visible. Our conscious awareness of this happening, our witnessing of life as revelation, is what makes life come alive with His presence. Mystics need to direct their attention to the world, recognizing the mystery of revelation in every corner of the world, especially where His presence is forgotten: the places of worldly power and greed. Even here, the secret substance of creation awaits attention, awaits its own awakening.

In our daily practice we bring this consciousness into our life, and the most direct way to do this is through love. Through the participation of this awakened consciousness in everyday life, the cellular structure of life is infused with a different frequency. The energy of divine awareness is given to life. The mystic knows how even the cells of her body are affected by her own awakening, how they praise Him more fully, how His love manifests more completely. The earth is also our body and all the cells of creation are linked together. Our awakening gives life joy, lets love flow freely, gives the world the seeds of its own remembrance.

LOVE WITHIN EMPTINESS

How do we help life awaken? We learn to bring love into the world. Our hearts can reflect That which is real into life, allowing His light and love to activate the secret substance within creation. Many of us confuse love with attachment, loving the objects of our desires, suffering from loss when those objects are gone. But real love is something else. Real love does not depend on possessing that which we desire. As we deepen our awareness of oneness, our experience of love changes. We come to know that love exists in the infinite space of our hearts, as well as in the finite forms of creation. In order to bring love into the world, we need to become more familiar with the love within emptiness, the love within silence. Then we can free ourselves from our attachments and allow love to flow where it is needed, rather than where we want it.

Silence is always present, hidden within everything. Yet often we turn away from silence, unable or unwilling to enter its space. Are we afraid of silence because in its emptiness there is no echo of who we are or would like to be? Are we afraid of silence because it does not belong to us, because it does not have borders or boundaries, substance or form? Or are we afraid because silence leaves us with nowhere to hide, and reveals that inside us which is empty?

Silence is permeated with love, singing with love. There is love that exists within forms, sounds, or activities. And there is love that is present in emptiness, in silence, in space. The love within silence does not demand recognition, but just is. This love belongs to the hidden face of God.

This world is the visible face of God, so full of beauty and wonder as well as tragedy and violence. But there is also His hidden nature, the secret aspect of the divine. His hidden essence is all around us, silent and empty. We cannot see it, hear it, touch it, but we can catch it for a moment, like a scent, invisible and yet present. In the undefined emptiness love flows freely, effortlessly, because there is no resistance; there are no power dynamics, no patterns of protection.

Mystics are trained to be awake in the emptiness, in the silence that is always present. In their own practice they awaken to the formless realms beyond the visible world. In Sufism, this process takes place through love of God. The lover is in love with an invisible Beloved, with That which cannot be named or defined. This mystical love works within the disciple, freeing her from the constrictions of form, immersing her in emptiness, in the dazzling darkness of what is Real.

Mystics become friends with the emptiness because they learn that the core of their own being is empty. Annihilation is not a battleground, but a place of prayer, a merging into That which is love Itself. Resistance belongs to the patterns of definition, to our limited sense of self. When we become conscious in the place where there is no resistance, love can flow and we can spread the wings of the heart. We can be where we are not, where only love is. In the words of the mad lover, Majnun, "Love has moved in and adorned the house. My self tied up its bundle and left."[2]

The nonexistence of the mystic is one of the secrets of the path. The mystical path takes us from being to nonbeing, a state of nonexistence that is dynamically alive and full of love. On the Sufi path this is the stage of *fanâ* that leads to *baqâ*, abiding in God. One can only abide in God in a state of nonexistence. Al-Junayd expresses this with paradoxical clarity:

> Being wholly present in God, he is wholly lost to self. And thus he is present before God, absent in himself; absent and present at the same time. He is where he is not and he is not where he is.[3]

As meditation and prayer pull us further into love's silence, the outer world can seem just a shell, a form without real substance. But this is only one stage on the journey, only part of love's cycle. If the mystic remained in a state of complete annihilation, she would be of no use in the world. Like the breath, love pulls us deep into nonexistence, and then returns us to outer life. We flow with His love and power from the world of form into the silence, and then again from the dimensions of emptiness back into life where we can be of use. Al-Junayd continues, describing how one returns from the state of complete *fanâ*:

Then after he has not been, he is where he is (before creation). He is himself, after he has not been truly himself. He is existent in himself and existent in God after having been existent in God and non-existent in himself. This is because he has left the drunkenness of God's overwhelming and come to the clarity of sobriety, and contemplation is once more restored to him, so that he can put everything in its right place and assess it correctly.[4]

The state of sobriety does not deny the experience of *fanâ*, but points to a state of being present and absent at the same time. Outwardly the mystic returns to the world of forms; inwardly she is absorbed in the nothingness. This enables her to function in the world while remaining inwardly free.

Mystics know that the world itself is a dance between existence and nonexistence. We embrace both His unknowable essence and the way His oneness is reflected into the world. His essence is hidden from the created world, "inaccessible and unknowable to every created thing always and forever."[5] Yet in the veils of creation that cover His face, He reveals Himself, His names and attributes.

Awake in emptiness and present in the world, the mystic can do the work of guiding love into life. Love comes into the world through the cycle of creation, the movement from nonexistence to existence. Love is the infinite ocean and yet is present in every touch, taste, and sound. It is hidden and revealed, continually flowing like the breath of God. It is in the movement of the stars and the way a flower opens to the dawn. And it is in the space between the stars, and between the flower and the sun.

Most people only find love in what is, in the touch of a friend or lover, in beautiful music, in a moment in nature. For an instant love becomes tangible, makes its presence felt, and we are nourished in ways we do not understand. We also feel the lack of love when we are denied, when something is not present. When our parent or partner does not give us what we want or need, we feel the pain of love's abandonment. And so we remain prisoners to the objects of love, forgetting that love itself is infinite and eternal.

The mystic who has tasted a love belonging to emptiness, who has drowned in love's infinite ocean, knows the invisible face of love. She knows of love's silence, love that does not belong to any form, is not identified with any source other than the infinite. Aware of her own essential emptiness, the mystic works with the emptiness of love, with the spaces where love flows freely. Because she is not attached to form, she can flow with love's flow, and she can be where she is not. She can work with love through all the planes of nonexistence and existence, reflecting His love where it is needed.

ONENESS AND MULTIPLICITY

Life needs love. In our drive to realize our ideals—technological as well as spiritual—we have turned away from what is simple and present. We have been working on the misconception that everyday life is of little spiritual value, that what we really long for is somewhere else. But the mystic knows that all the world is a reflection of the oneness of God, that everything is included in His love.

The energy of creation flows from nonbeing into being, from emptiness into form. Nonbeing comes into being through a single point of oneness that contains the existence of the whole in potential. From this place life explodes into multiplicity, into all the forms and colors of creation, revealing the single face of God in different hues. As Einstein suggested, the infinite energies of the universe all burst forth from one tiny point. What scientists don't understand is that this process didn't just happen once. Existence is born again and again—thousands of times in every moment. Oneness and multiplicity are in a continual dance, a constant and endless process of creation.

Because our consciousness is conditioned by linear, sequential thought patterns based on a perspective of duality, we tend to see each stage of creation as separate. We assume the state of oneness is left behind as soon as multiplicity is born. This perspective separates creation from the Creator. But from a perspective of oneness, all different levels and aspects of reality are interdependent. Multiplicity and oneness, relative and absolute, being and nonbeing—all levels interpenetrate and reflect each other. Mystical experiences reveal this dynamic relationship—"Wheresoever you turn, there is the face of God."

The relationship between oneness and multiplicity is one of the secrets of creation. All of the changing forms of life arise within this dance. And the relationship between oneness and multiplicity is not fixed. It has the potential to evolve, to change its patterns of revelation. This is one of the forces behind what we call evolution. Our culture has conditioned us to see life only from the surface. We have lost touch with the mystery of things, with the forces that work in the unseen. But within oneness there is a consciousness that determines the patterns of manifestation, that guides the way the many reflect the face of the One.

And this consciousness is not separate from life. It belongs to life's interrelated whole. Just as the Higher Self is not separate from the individual but permeates the whole person, so too does this consciousness permeate all of life. In this universal Self we are all connected. It is present in each of us, and uses the consciousness of humanity to express itself. Humanity now has the potential to work with this consciousness of oneness. If we work with the consciousness of oneness that is within life, we can help something new be born in the relationship between creation and the Creator. We can help manifest a new step in evolution in which all life awakens within a new relationship with the divine.

LOVE AND THE WEB OF LIFE

All of life is woven together in an endlessly flowing web of energy. Spiritual traditions have always recognized the truth of interdependence, the essential interconnectedness of all existence. Separation is an illusion; all things connect together within a greater wholeness.

Ecologists as well as mystics understand the oneness that is at the core of life. Scientists know that when a butterfly flaps its wings in one part of the world, it can affect weather patterns across the globe. But this is a one-dimensional view. It acknowledges that all life is interconnected, but does not address the potential for real change. Spiritual evolution occurs when something higher enters into existence, when something from the inner planes passes through all levels and helps establish a new dynamic between creation and the source of creation.

The ways the One manifests within creation change; the ways life relates to the source of life change. The evolutionary potential of this time is for the oneness of life to be infused with a new consciousness. This is already happening. Something new has been given, something that can help the oneness of life vibrate with a higher frequency of divine presence. But how can we recognize and receive what has been given?

The most direct way to participate in God's revelation of His oneness in the world is through love, because love belongs to oneness. Love gives just as it receives; it knows no boundaries, and flows where it is needed. Love brings us together and awakens our awareness of how we belong to each other as well as to what is Real. Love itself is the core of creation's relationship with its Creator.

Love always draws us to oneness, whether in a personal relationship or a relationship with God in the depths of silence. Love awakens our longing for oneness, and it also carries the knowing of oneness. The mystic has always worked with this knowing in which the façade of the world, the dance of appearances, is permeated with a light that reflects its deeper meaning. This light is a knowing of love and a knowing of oneness. Without it life is just a reflection of shadows, moving images that have little value. With this knowing, we can read the book of life; we can understand the true nature of our experiences. No longer caught in the duality of how things appear, the opposites of good or bad, pleasure or pain, we are able to see into the deeper meaning of life reflected in the mirror of the heart. In the interrelated pattern that underlies all of life, nothing is excluded. Life is always beckoning, drawing us deeper into ourself.

Love awakens us and speaks to us, using its many voices. How we respond to life depends upon our openness to love, to this essence that is all around us. Love is not just a feeling between people, but an energy that is present in everything. Love is in the darkness and the violence, as well as in the beauty and the bliss. In love nothing is excluded, because love belongs to oneness. The intensity of this inclusion can be too much for some people, who prefer to protect themselves with partitions, to exclude what they do not like, what they cannot easily understand. But the strength of love is that it is not limited to forms, to ideals, or to patterns of behavior. It is always present and always free. Without love the atoms would not spin, the earth would not circle the sun.

To work with love is to put aside the preconceptions of the mind, the prejudices of conditioning. The knowing of love belongs to the highest parts of ourself, not to our personality. This knowing is not just a spiritual ideal, but a practical way to live and understand. The heart as an organ of perception has a clarity that is rarely found in the mind. Emotions and feelings may cloud our perceptions, but within the core of our being are a directness and simplicity that belong to Truth. If we are able to live from this core, then the knowing of love directs our life and uncovers the deeper purpose of everyday life.

How can we bring the simplicity and clarity of love into our outer life? By recognizing that it is already present. The mystic knows that everything is the face of God. But so often we forget, and our forgetfulness isolates us. We live without this knowing, without its potency to uncover life's secrets. We think we are here to fulfill our own purpose, and we forget that we are here for His sake. This deeper meaning in our life is inaccessible: we only have the distortions of our own story, the ramblings of the ego. But if we can remember that life needs our presence, that love needs our heart, then a different story becomes visible. In this story we are no longer the central figure, but part of a vaster drama that is written by the hand of God.

Love—simple, always present and yet paradoxically hidden and often seemingly inaccessible—is our essence. Love connects all of life together. And in these connections the blueprints of our survival are written. Love brings things together in an ever-evolving web that cannot be prescribed or controlled. This web within all life is what needs to be made conscious, and it is the knowing of love that can reveal its deeper meaning.

WORKING WITH THE WEB OF LIFE

The web of life has been a mystical secret for centuries. But now it is being awakened. It is being given a quality of consciousness that belongs to the next stage of humanity's evolution and the evolution of the whole planet. The possibility of this awakening means that all of life can become more conscious of its interrelatedness and its relationship with the source. Love is key to this process, because without love the oneness of life would be mechanical. We could recognize our essential interdependence, but what does this mean? Buddhism answered this question in the teachings of the second turning of the wheel of *dharma*, which recognized that reality is not simply empty but contains a quality of luminosity and love that reveals the oneness of all life. With this shift was born Mahayana Buddhism, and the tradition of the *bodhisattvas* whose compassionate presence serves all beings.

Meaning comes from love, from the consciousness of love that reveals our connection to each other and engenders compassion, involvement, and responsibility to the whole. What would it matter if a consciousness of oneness were awakened without the wisdom of compassion and service?

The web of life is being charged with a new quality of love in order to help us make our next step. It is being magnetically aligned with the hearts of humanity, so that they can directly influence and support each other across the planet. A new thread of love that contains a consciousness of oneness is being woven into the fabric of the world. A new color in the spectrum of love is being made visible. It was always present, but until now it has been hidden. Now it can be accessible to all of us. The web of life needs the vibration of this quality of love in order to awaken humanity, in order for love's essential oneness to be known. Without this vibration of love there can be no evolution in consciousness; there would be no container for the soul of the world to be born.

Like the breath, the cycle of love endlessly flows between the worlds. Love comes from the Creator, from the indefinable, unknowable Essence, into the world of manifestation. And every cell of creation is a celebration of this love, an offering of itself back to the Creator. This is the mystical truth of "He loves them and they love Him." Most people only experience love when it hits the plane of manifestation, when the creation mirrors the Creator. But mystics who belong to both, the unmanifest and manifest worlds, can experience the whole cycle of love within themselves. They experience the infinite emptiness, the dazzling darkness where there is no reflection, only pure undifferentiated love. They can also sense the joy of creation as it participates in manifesting His love, in expressing love in so many different forms and colors. And in the polished surface of their own heart they directly experience the wonder of reflecting His love. In this moment of reflection they participate in the mystery of Him making Himself known to Himself. The lover can consciously participate in the revelation of His love.

The web of life is woven into this cycle of love. His lovers hold the consciousness of this web within their hearts. Without the presence of the hearts of His lovers in the world, the web of life would not carry the meaning of His presence. An indefinable essence would be absent and the colors would fade away. We belong to love more than we are aware.

Mystics have completed the work of creating the container of light around the world that can allow love to flow into the web of life. This container, this web of light, is vibrating with the energy of the new era. It has a quality of completeness that has not been seen before, and it is accessible to anyone who turns her attention away from the desires of the ego, into her love for what is Real. How do we take this step? When we acknowledge that we do not belong only to ourselves, but that we belong in the oneness that is present in all life, then what is needed can be given.

Like many spiritual steps this is simple but not easy. There are few complications and yet we like to make things complicated. We like to invent difficulties to keep us busy, to keep our attention away from the real work. But the simple practice is to recognize that we do not belong to ourselves. We are here for the sake of something else. Many spiritual traditions have been subverted into some form of self-fulfillment, some image of progress. But real spiritual work requires the basic understanding that it is not about us, about our own progress or achievement. Each moment is an opportunity to remember God, to open ourselves to love for His sake.

The awakened heart of a lover of God is the most efficient way to bring love into the midst of life. Our inner attention aligns our consciousness with love as it comes into the world. Love carries the knowledge of where it needs to go, the direction it needs to take. But it needs our own alignment in order to make this happen. Otherwise love cannot flow freely; a dissonance happens on the inner plane that impedes its flow and distorts its direction.

Through our spiritual practices we are trained to be inwardly focused. We are trained to be attentive in both the outer and inner world. Outer attention connects us with His presence in the world. Learning to be attentive where there are no forms enables us to be attuned with the energy of love before it comes into manifestation. Through our meditation and remembrance we are awake in emptiness. The absence of the mystic enables her to work with the undefined essence of love in the inner worlds, in dimensions that are fluid and not fixed into form. While her attentive presence in daily life connects her to the web of life, her inner state of absence can connect her to the source of love.

Love needs our inner purity and emptiness of intention in order to bring its knowing into life. The moment we try to condition love, to determine its form or way of expression, we limit its potential. The emptiness of the mystic is a practical vehicle for love to do its work. This emptiness is a state of dynamic attention, requiring our full participation. Through our conscious participation, love can use our consciousness. Through our complete surrender to this process, love can use the full potential of our divinity. Through the simple practices of remembrance and attention in our daily life, the energy of love is woven into the web of life.

The web of life carries the song of humanity, the song of the soul of the world. It is protected by the power of our devotion and the presence of the masters of love. This song is also present in the spinning hearts of the lovers of God, in those who have given their life to this

work. Gradually this song is being brought into consciousness. The web of life is telling us the story of our
own destiny. Life in all its forms is imprinted with
meaning, and this meaning is coming alive in a new way.
We have forgotten why we are here, but life is mirroring
to us the meaning written in our hearts. The difference
between living and being alive is an awareness of this
meaning, an awareness of this song of love. For each of
us this song is unique, and yet the song of the whole of
humanity, of all life, of the entire world, is also our own
song. In the unfolding of oneness this is not a paradox,
but a simple expression of how oneness works.

AWAKENING LIFE

Within the chemistry of life are cells waiting to be activated by love. They are nodes of power within the web
of life. They carry the blueprint of life's transformation.
If they are not awakened, they will remain dormant and
a possibility will have passed. They need to be awakened
in a certain order so that the awakening energy flows in
a specific way. This is similar to the energy centers in an
individual, which should never be randomly activated.
The cellular structure of life and its flowing web of energy are a careful balance of light and dark, positive and
negative. Infusing too much energy into this structure
can easily upset this balance. This is why there are such
dangers at any time of transformation and why the work
requires such careful attention.

Working with the web of life requires a more conscious presence in the world, a mystical orientation
towards being. The emptiness, the silence are always
with us, but the focus of the lover needs to shift towards

divine presence. Our attention in the world has the clarity that can only come from inner emptiness, from nonattachment to form. We can work with the web of life free from personal desires. Then our love will go where it is needed and our divine consciousness interact with life's chemistry.

With each breath we are bonded with life. With each repetition of His name divine remembrance is imprinted into life. As we move from an attitude of separation to a consciousness of oneness with life, life will respond. We will come to know the degree of our interconnection, how our consciousness flows out into life along the energy patterns of creation. We will see how subtly our consciousness interacts with life, and how our own transformation affects the whole. We will also become more attuned to the need of the world. The world will speak to us in a new way, following the paths of oneness that are imprinted into our brain but at present unused.

Love flows through all life and love spins the heart. The spinning of the heart takes us beyond the limited vision of the mind into the vaster dimensions of our real being. Love awakens us, frees us from the prison of our ego-self. Love can also awaken the world. When the web of life starts to spin with the frequency of the consciousness of love and oneness, the world can begin to awaken to its real nature. One friend had a dream that pointed to this awakening as an image of a child:

> In my arms I was holding a beautiful and luminous child. It was not a child of the flesh and blood, but a child whose surface of light and stars seemed wrapped about an interior of emptiness, of space. And yet this child was an organic, living being,

inspiring incredible tenderness and awe. I was so amazed.

This child whose surface is of light and stars also belongs to life, is an organic, living being. "As above, so below" is a saying of the alchemists who worked with the transformation of matter. They knew the correspondences between the worlds, and the secrets of light hidden in matter. Immersed in matter, we have forgotten its transformative potential.

In the consciousness of love lie the secrets of transformation. When this consciousness is given to the world, the work of transformation can begin. Slowly, the world can awaken, its magic come alive again.

LIFE'S INTERCONNECTION

Tie yourself to everything in creation
That got poured from God's magic hat.

O, tie your soul like a magnificent sweet chime
To every leaf and limb in existence.

Hafiz[1]

THE WHOLENESS OF LIFE

Life is complete. Different levels of reality interconnect within life. The planes of nonbeing, the dimension of pure oneness and pure consciousness, and all the different levels of manifestation from the archetypal to the physical interpenetrate each other. Nothing is separate. Each level of reality is present in each moment of existence. And human beings are unique in the pattern of creation in that all these levels are present within us and accessible to our consciousness. We can embrace the physical plane and dissolve into nonbeing. We can be present in pure consciousness, interact with the imaginal reality of the archetypal world, and function in the mental world of thoughts.

From the perspective of life's oneness, there is no separation, no hierarchy, and no ladder of ascent; rather there are patterns of interconnection and movements of energy. Energy forms into matter or constellates into images. Life expresses itself in so many ways, each mode having its purpose and meaning, each aspect of creation reflecting the whole in a unique way. The relationship of the one to the many, of the individual to the whole, will be the science of the future. Our understanding of the way energy moves between different levels of reality will give us access to a fuller understanding of life and how to work with life's energy.

Science has shown us that the world is not the solid, three-dimensional reality that our senses imagine. As we awaken to the ways energy moves between different levels of reality, we will be able to work with the secrets of creation. And we will begin to perceive how our consciousness affects the whole, how our perception determines our experience. Just as Newtonian physics gave us some understanding of how the forces in the physical world interact, the science of the future will offer a knowledge of oneness, revealing not only the patterns of oneness in this world, but how the different worlds interpenetrate and affect each other, and how our consciousness plays a central role in their interaction.

In order to begin to access the knowledge of oneness and accept our responsibilities within life, we need to leave behind our focus on self-preservation at the expense of the whole. Our concepts of separation and individual progress are creating a field of self-destruction. As we focus on our own needs, whether individual or national, we block the light and energy that should be flowing through our consciousness into the whole of life, and life is left barren.

Life needs a certain energy in order to flourish and transform. This energy must flow through human beings because only then can it carry the vibration of conscious purpose that is needed. A higher consciousness has always played a part in the evolution of life, helping to direct its patterns of change. This has always been part of humanity's role on the earth, but this conscious direction has been held in trust for humanity by the spiritual masters who are with us. The Confucian Doctrine of the Mean reflects this relationship:

> Only those who are absolutely sincere can fully develop their nature. If they can fully develop their nature, they can fully develop the nature of others. If they can fully develop the nature of others, they can fully develop the nature of things. If they can fully develop the nature of things, they can then assist in the transforming and nourishing process of Heaven and Earth.[2]

Throughout time, spiritual traditions have pointed to the role of human beings in the mystery of revelation, in the coming together of heaven and earth. But now what has been the conscious work of the few is being given back to the whole of humanity. We all have the opportunity to accept a greater responsibility within the unfolding of life.

We have many cultural and psychological patterns that encourage us to avoid the responsibilities that are given to us. We prefer to remain as children. We have even characterized our relationship to the divine as a child's relationship to its parent, with a divine father or mother image. This creates feelings of safety and security. But if we look around us we see the illusory nature of these feelings. We are not secure, and life is not safe. The destiny of our planet hangs in the balance. We cannot afford to play the part of children any more. We may not want to take responsibility for the destiny of our planet, but that is what is being given back to us.

Accepting our responsibilities means that we can no longer rely on outer authorities. The mediocrity of our present world leaders, their lack of real vision, is evident, but we don't want to realize the full significance of that fact. It points not just to the corruption of our political systems, but to a deeper transition in which the real potential is being given to the individual. This is part of the shift from a hierarchical model of power and information exchange to a model of organic wholeness through which the energy of our time needs to flow.

This is so different from our present image of the decision-making process that we cannot even imagine how it could work. But we are beginning to see a collective awakening to the truth that we cannot look for any savior outside ourself. Neither a political nor a spiritual leader is coming to redeem us. The development of individual consciousness is pushing us to take real responsibility for life—not just for our individual life, but for the life of the whole.

THE KNOWING OF LOVE

Love contains a consciousness that can help us look away from ourselves and towards the needs of the whole. Love is present everywhere at the same time. This is one of the secrets of love that is hidden from ordinary consciousness. Our individual experience of love may be determined by the openness of our heart and other criteria, but love itself is not localized. Working with love, we have access to its totality of presence. When our focus is towards our individual self we see only fragments of love, but when we turn away from ourself we can glimpse its vaster dimension. When we work with a heart and mind that are not controlled by self-interest, we can have direct access to the oneness that is within all of life.

When we are present in love, love speaks to us. The heart's knowing is not governed by the mind, and yet the mind can learn to grasp it. In the knowing of love, the interconnections of life are directly accessible. Love knows what is needed in every situation. Love has its own language, its signs and symbols. Love comes to us in its own way, and part of the training of the lover is to learn the ways of love, to learn its silence and speech, to learn to be patient and wait for love, and then respond with immediate attention. The consciousness of the heart, the place where love speaks to us, is always unconditioned, because real love is fundamentally free. That is why so many people are frightened of love: it frees us from the security of our defenses and conditioning, from our patterns of control.

Identifying love as just a feeling between people, we have lost touch with its vaster potential, with its all-embracing nature. Focusing on our personal need for love, we cannot see how it can connect us to the whole, for the sake of the whole. Even many schools of contemporary spirituality look only at love's personal qualities, often identifying it with emotional needs. But love is an energy source of unlimited potential that carries the consciousness of the whole.

Buddhist traditions reflect the impersonal nature of love as they describe Reality as a combination of vast emptiness and compassion. The Third Karmapa of Tibetan Buddhism wrote,

> The play of overwhelming compassion being
>   unobstructed,
> In the moment of love
> The empty essence nakedly dawns.[3]

Buddhism shows us that love is not some idealized romance but a practical and potent power that is part of the essence of the universe. It needs us to be awake and attentive, watchful and present, and forgetful of our own self. Then it can take us into the arena of oneness where the secrets of life are being made visible. When we rest in the nature of what is Real, we relate skillfully in the world for the sake of all beings.

The first step in working with the consciousness of love is to realize the limitations of our personal preoccupation with love. Of course we all want to be loved. This is a basic human instinct. We cannot ignore or repress this need, but it does not have to dominate our attitude. The lover of Truth has a deeper need: to give her heart in service to what is Real. The lover is in service to love, rather than love's being in service to her. This fundamental shift in attitude is what opens us to love's real nature. Love can then speak to us and explain how it works. Love can open us to its vaster dimension in which all of life is present.

The focus of many mystical traditions has been on the way love unites the individual with the divine. This is one of love's most precious qualities, creating a longing for union, for being dissolved in love and the emptiness of love. Love takes us away from ourself into the presence of the Real. But love also reveals the wonder of divine oneness in the world. Love helps us to see the face of God wheresoever we turn. Love allows us to participate in life from the place of oneness, to experience life without the distortions of duality. Love can open the door to life in its completeness, in the wonder of its wholeness, in its beauty and majesty. Love gives us the freedom and power to live.

When we come to know the real potentials of love, we can help direct it where it is needed. Love knows our own true nature and uses it for the benefit of the whole. We can bring divine awareness into places where it has been forgotten—to the boardrooms that are only interested in profit, to the refugee camps that foster hatred. We can follow love as it flows within the patterns of creation, making our own small contribution. In our inner practice and outer life our attention is taken where it can help, where the consciousness of divine presence can unblock life's energy, where remembrance can purify, where devotion can bring warmth.

Yet there is also resistance to this unfolding of love. This is the battle of light and darkness that is taking place. In our personal practice we know the resistance to remembrance, how the ego interferes with our devotion, how our conditioning denies us our freedom. The same is true on a global scale, except that the forces of resistance are more dangerous. On the inner planes these forces are like dark walls resistant to change, places where the light cannot easily penetrate. They control much of our economy and commerce: the buying and selling of goods and also of human beings. And they are not static, but want to dominate and expand their control.

This is where those who want nothing for themselves—who love only the Truth—are needed. These forces of self-interest are threatened by the power of love, which brings freedom without hierarchy or ideology. The potency of love is that it cannot be limited, cannot be controlled. Love also antagonizes the dominance of the mind and its constructs. Love moves faster than the mind. It can subvert the most sensible process.

Encountering the resistance to love, the servant knows that all is according to His will. There is a deeper wholeness in which even the resistance plays its part. Light and dark move together, and the resistance to love draws our attention into the darkness, into the places of contraction where we are needed. We know this process within our own psyche, how our darkness draws us deeper within, into places that have been forgotten and neglected, that carry the scars of abuse. The same can happen in the way the resistance to love can carry us into the heart of darkness, to the places in the energy structure of the world where He has been most forgotten or violated. Love draws our attention where it is needed, and the attention of the lover carries the consciousness of the oneness of God. Just as His name can untangle the blocks of our own psyche, so can our attention, imprinted with His name, work to free the energy patterns of life. Silently, through love and devotion, the healing of the world can take place.

WORKING WITH THE FLOW OF LOVE

Because all of life is interdependent, removing energy blocks in one part of life allows energy to flow into and transform other parts. All we have to do to affect the energy patterns of the whole is to be attentive wherever we are needed. One of the results of global communication is that we know where there are trouble and suffering in the world; our conscious attention can immediately focus on these areas. We do not have to do anything except be aware—the attention of those who have stepped aside from their own self-interest is a tremendous force.

Surrendered in service, we know that we are where we are needed, and that our inner attention and prayers are used for the good of the whole. We see life's wholeness around us and know that even in the ordinariness of our daily life we are not isolated from the suffering of others. This does not mean we identify with their suffering. Our compassion is a force of healing in itself. Compassion's wisdom recognizes the way the soul is purified by pain, the way the divine can reveal itself through suffering. The attention of the heart brings light into darkness, giving sustenance to those in need.

This work takes attention but no time, as love does not belong to time or to space. The immediacy of global communication mirrors the immediacy of love. We no longer have to wait to reach others. The glance of the lover, the inner attention of the heart, directs the consciousness of love where it is needed in the moment.

The work of love is never forced. It is a natural part of life. It is common sense. We care for neighbors and friends, for all of humanity, for we are part of the same community. We do not try to do anything, because that would be imposing our will. We live our ordinary, everyday life, open to life's interconnections. As we live with the global awareness that is becoming more and more present, our individual consciousness becomes more attuned to the consciousness of the world.

During the last millennia the focus of many spiritual traditions has been on the inner journey of the individual, the solitary path of the soul back to God. In contemporary Western spirituality, this has been combined with our preoccupation with individual fulfillment. But the focus on the individual journey has not always been the primal spiritual emphasis. In previous eras spiritual training was more concerned with the well-being of the tribe or the whole, as is still reflected in the role of the shaman. Martin Prechtel makes this comment in his experience of the Mayans:

The New Age falls pretty flat with the Mayans because, to them, self discovery is good only if it helps to feed the whole.[4]

In the Mahayana Buddhist traditions, the quest for realization is intertwined with the *bodhisattva* ideal of service to all beings. The *bodhisattva* vow taken by many practitioners commits one to returning to this plane of existence until all beings have attained enlightenment. On the Sufi path the road to union with God leads to the state of servanthood. Sufis are known as "the slaves of the One and servants of the many." And there has always been the tradition of the *awliya*, the friends of God, who look after the well-being of humanity.

It is time now to return to this emphasis on paths that are in service to the whole. Experiencing the union of the soul with Reality is always the primary stamp of the mystic. But our perspective on this mystery can change and evolve. As our collective consciousness becomes more attuned to a global awareness, the mystic can also bring this perspective into her work of reflecting what is Real into the world. The lover can see how she can participate more fully with the whole, how she can give herself more completely to the life of the One.

By giving herself to God, the lover gives herself to life. If we believe in His oneness, there is nothing other than God. In the words of Abu Sa'id ibn Abî-l-Khayr,

Sufism consists in turning the heart away from anything that is not God. But there is not anything that is not God.

Living this oneness unites our inner practice with our service to life. However, our culture's reliance on rational thought is an obstacle to living from a place of oneness. We are used to approaching the difficulties of the world with solely a linear, analytic attitude. The ways of oneness cannot reveal themselves through rational thought, because rational analysis tends to separate the parts from the whole, thereby losing the greater perspective.

If we look to life with a consciousness of love as well as rationality, oneness will open its doors. The secrets of life's oneness will become visible. The oneness of love within our heart will interact with the oneness within all of life and reveal to us the way oneness works in the world. Without this new knowledge, humanity cannot evolve from its present predicament. We have been given some of the tools of oneness in the form of global communication, but we do not know how to use them. We see their function in terms of the individual. We do not know how to let oneness speak to us, interact with us. We still see ourselves as separate from life. Through the light of oneness we will be able to see the larger picture, and learn how to work with what we have been given.

The mystic knows that what we need is always present, but we have to transform our awareness. We need the humility to be taught how to see our own world afresh. For the Sufi life is always the greatest teacher. Life will reveal to us what we need to know. His oneness imprinted into our heart will interact with the oneness present in life. Our own direct perception of nonduality, of belonging to what is Real, can infuse the currents of oneness that flow through life, and a new way will be born into consciousness.

ACCEPTING RESPONSIBILITY

With each step in the development of consciousness there is always a sacrifice. We understand this as individuals; we know how at every stage of the path something is lost. Consciousness itself demands the loss of innocence, the expulsion from paradise. In order to embrace a consciousness of the whole, we have to surrender our illusion of autonomy. The idea that the individual has the possibility or right to determine her own life is one of the hallmarks of our culture. It gives us the illusion of freedom and self-determinacy.

The evolution of consciousness always means more responsibility, and increased responsibility often appears as a loss of freedom. The adolescent who steps into adulthood and becomes responsible for others in his family or community may feel the pain of an apparent loss. But real responsibility gives us the freedom to participate in life in ways that are closed to adolescent self-centeredness.

Western culture, which clings to the idea of independence rather than embracing the reality of interdependence, has the quality of an adolescent who refuses to accept the effects of his actions. This pattern is visible in our national politics, as well as in the principles that ground our free-market economy. What we do not realize is that this inability to accept responsibility for our actions not only has negative global repercussions, but blocks us from accessing powers that belong to us. With each step in maturity we are given access to another level of our human potential. The illusion of autonomy— whether individual or national—constricts us within the sphere of our own limited power.

The shift towards maturity will allow us to reconnect with life with an attitude of inclusion: the different parts are acknowledged as belonging together. This fundamental shift in attitude allows life to communicate itself to us more directly. This is not an ideological approach but a way of life that recognizes the oneness that is inherent in creation and within us. This simple step will allow our consciousness to function on a different frequency, one that is much faster and more efficient. And most important, on this frequency we are directly and consciously connected to all of life.

Our individual consciousness has the capacity to function in this way: to see each part in relationship to the whole. Through the dynamics of oneness we will come to understand the way each individual part relates to the whole, just as we are now preoccupied with analyzing how individual parts interact with each other. We will come to understand the laws of economics as well as the laws of nature from a perspective of wholeness.

NEW CENTERS OF ENERGY

When we collectively accept our global responsibilities, energy will begin to flow through the conscious interrelationship between the individual and the whole, spinning a new form of wisdom into existence. The energy that can only come from a lived understanding of wholeness will activate certain energy centers in life that have been dormant. And the individual is a microcosm of the whole. Just as energy centers in life will be activated, so too will patterns in the brain that now exist only in a state of potential.

The release of energy and knowledge from these centers will change life as we know it, enabling a different level of evolution to take place. Only then will we begin to understand our place within the galaxy and the flow of forces that interact with our planet. We are not an isolated planet whose unique chemical mixture gave birth to life, but part of a dynamic outpouring of love and energy throughout the universe. The universe is a living wholeness whose forces and energy patterns flow and interact. The mystic who has stepped beyond the confines of the ego has glimpsed this vastness of our real nature. Our concept of our planet as the entirety of existence is as limited and mistaken as our identifying ourselves as our egos. Astrology and astronomy point to the influence of other planets on our individual life, but there are also more powerful and more distant forces at play, whose influence we have yet to discover and understand.

Focused on our individual self, we remain isolated, and our consciousness can only assimilate knowledge that reflects this attitude. As we accept the wholeness of creation, creation can speak to us in the language of wholeness. Our consciousness can then expand to assimilate a horizon not delineated by self-interest. The mystic knows that consciousness can expand and expand, that its potential is unlimited. We are made in the image of God and carry His unlimited potential within us. Taking responsibility for our planet, we will begin to see our place within the larger framework of our galaxy. The knowledge that belongs to this stage of our evolution can then be given to us.

If we can recognize that life wants to teach us, we can take the next step in the development of consciousness. Human beings belong to all of life, and creation needs our attention, our participation. The simplicity of our relationship to life is overwhelming. Life, the eco-system, is not a complex problem to be solved. It is a living organism that needs to be related to. Through this relationship life can use our consciousness to untangle the knots and imbalances that we have caused through our ignorance. As the Biblical prophet Hosea so accu-rately describes our time, "There is ... no knowledge of God in the land.... Therefore the land mourns."[5] With-out our conscious participation, the knowledge of divine oneness that we hold in our hearts will never nourish the planet, and we will limit the next step in our collective evolution.

CONNECTING LEVELS OF REALITY

The inner and outer worlds come together in the human being. Different levels of reality that exist within us are mirrored in the outer world. The vastness of our inner emptiness is reflected in the vastness of outer space. Mystical experiences can show us how the ego is like a small planet in endless space; coming back from the beyond and entering the ego is like landing again on this planet. Suddenly one is present in a reality—with personal problems or collective difficulties—which a moment ago seemed so insignificant. But then one discovers a different purpose emerging, a purpose that combines the vastness of the infinite with our presence in this world. Recently a friend had an experience that pointed to this:

> I felt in the night while I was sleeping that I was drawn out of my body while fully conscious, in a kind of very long and very thin channel. Then I

lost physical, emotional, and mental consciousness, and was thrown with an unbelievable speed
into the infinite emptiness, whirled around in
intergalactic spaces. It was such freedom, being
without identity. There was Nothingness, yet it
was very dynamic. Then there was this enormous
field of energy of the Brotherhood, the Helpers of
humanity, our spiritual ancestors. They made ab-
solutely clear that our connection to them is to be
brought down to earth through us and that this is
needed for the world situation.

When the friend awoke, she knew the importance
of this experience. She wrote, "And may I never forget
for one moment what I was shown! Just through the
connection, through them and then through us, what is
needed can be given. It was absolute; truth. With the
grace of the Beloved never will it be forgotten." The
friend was taken into the infinite emptiness where the
masters of love are present, and then she was shown the
meaning of our connection with their energy field, how
it is needed in the world. This connection allows energy,
love, and knowledge to flow from one level of reality to
another. This has always been the way humanity has
been helped. But in order to live this connection, it is
necessary to step out of the ego and embrace a vaster
dimension of consciousness. Otherwise the doubts and
distortions of the mind will destroy the connection and
nothing can be given. This is not spiritual science fiction
but the way the world has always functioned.

The masters of love need their servants in the world
who can be present and yet have the experience of inner
realities where we are absent to self. In the intergalactic
spaces of infinite emptiness there are pure love, wisdom,

power. There are forces waiting to help us. We are working together as part of an opening of love that is so vast and full of so many miracles. And yet the insignificance of our ordinary self has a part to play. We are needed by love. Through us the higher frequencies of love and oneness can interpenetrate the world.

CREFLECTIONS of LIGHT

O Light of light, Thy light illuminates the people of heaven
and enlightens the people of earth.
O Light of all light. Thy light is praised by all light.

Prayer attributed to Mohammed

RADIANT AND REFLECTED LIGHT

In the dimension of pure consciousness, on the plane of
the Self, things are known by their light.[1] Here, everything radiates a quantity and quality of light unique to
its essential nature. On this plane human beings are like
suns, their light shining as stars in space.

But this dimension of light is hidden from ordinary
consciousness. In the physical realm of the senses we live
in a world of shadows. The pure light of our true existence is veiled. This realm is a place of reflection, in which
we see objects not through their own light, but through
the light that is reflected off them. With no external
source of light, physical objects are in the dark, invisible.
And the colors that we perceive in this world are not the
actual colors of the objects but the colors that are reflected
off them. Grass absorbs light except for the frequency
equivalent to the color green, which is reflected back.
Black absorbs all colors; white reflects all colors. In this
world we rarely perceive things according to their true
nature.

Our interaction with this world is governed by the laws of reflection. Reflections are full of distortions and ambiguity, full of shadows. In this world it is difficult to perceive or experience things directly. In human interaction we are also confronted by the reflection of our own self, much more than we would like to admit. We perceive and interact with others according to our own psychological patterns and conditioning. In the realm of pure consciousness it is very different: there we relate essence to essence. There is no reflection, but an interaction of light upon light, a meeting, merging, and dynamic interplay of light.

On the inner planes there are also places of shadows and darkness, places where there is little light. There are forces of darkness, forces that deny the light. There are entities that absorb rather than radiate light, creating darkness. These entities are like black holes whose density is so great that no light escapes. Human beings rarely interact or are present in these places, although these loci can influence us. The true nature of human beings is light, and our light protects us from darkness. In our world misunderstandings and discord usually arise from the distortions caused by the reflections of light. The more we have access to the realm of pure consciousness, the more clearly we can see. The work of the masters of love and their helpers is to give us as much light as we can absorb without being blinded or unbalanced.

On the plane of pure consciousness light flows directly: there is no distortion or reflection. Light radiates from each source and communicates through this radiance. In this realm things are known by their similarities rather than defined by their differences. Similar frequencies of light resonate together and attract each other. There is no space or time, but there are loci, or different realms, in this dimension. Just as light has different frequencies, so too are there different levels within the dimension of light where those with similar frequencies of light are attracted. The different levels of light function at slightly different speeds.

Most human beings remain in the level of light to which they belong. Their soul functions at this particular frequency. However, there are spiritual trainings that enable individuals to function at different levels, to move between frequencies of light. These individuals also have the capacity to bring light to different places, even to realms of shadows and darkness. Their work is to bring light to where it is needed.

On the inner planes light can move freely. The difficulty comes in bringing light into the world of reflection, which requires great care and precision. Just as our physical world needs the ozone layer to protect it from the negative effects of too much sunlight, so do we need to be protected against the direct light of pure being. In this world of reflection, Truth would blind us, just as pure love burns us. The direct light of pure being has to be gradually infused into our world.

At times of transition, energy is required to fuel and facilitate change. In psychological transformation this energy usually comes from the unconscious, often causing turmoil in one's inner and outer life as old patterns are disrupted or destroyed. This energy is sometimes imaged in dreams by snakes, earthquakes, or other symbols.

Spiritual transformation requires a different energy to which spiritual paths and their practices give us access. At a certain level these transformations are so delicate and dangerous that a master is needed to guide the process. If one is given too much energy one can become unbalanced, too little energy and the transformation does not take place or happens at a lower level. And because each individual is structured slightly differently, this energy has to be given according to one's individual nature. This is one of the reasons why one needs a spiritual guide.

The work of global transformation is even more subtle and delicate. Energy is required to enable this transformation, but any time a quantity of energy comes from a different dimension there is the danger of imbalance. A certain degree of imbalance is inevitable—this is one of the signs of transformation as old structures lose their stability. But if forces start to spin out of control, it can be disastrous. The work is to bring the right amount of energy into the world in the right places and to ensure that it is contained and reflected to where it is needed.

The web of light and love that has been created around the world will enable this to happen, but due to continually shifting needs and circumstances, the structure of the web needs to be constantly altered. Different spiritual groups are involved in this work, which requires much careful attention. The more these groups work together, the more easily the energy can flow. Until now this co-operation has taken place mainly on the inner planes. But there is an increasing need for this global work to be made conscious in the outer world. It is becoming necessary for us to know in this world the work that we are doing together.

As energy comes from the inner world, the most dangerous moment is when it hits the plane of reflection. In the inner dimensions it flows freely without the dynamic of cause and effect. We are where we are needed at each moment: there is no transition or temporal dynamic. Essence relates to essence without the danger of distortion. Coming into this world, the energy enters a reality governed by different laws. Here there is action and reaction, the interplay of light and shadows. Here there are also the subtleties of time and the effects of physical place. And most important, there is the inconsistency of people. There is no absolute knowing what kind of effect the energy of light will have. Unless one is completely surrendered in service, there will be some kind of reaction to the energy. We are free to accept or reject what is offered; as human beings we have free will. But whatever course we choose, the light will affect us. We react to divine light and love far more than we are aware.

CONSCIOUSNESS AND LIGHT

Light moves through human beings from the higher dimensions to the lower. Human beings have the capacity to transmute light, to make it accessible at a lower frequency. Usually this is done unknowingly, just as a plant transmutes sunlight in the process of photosynthesis. Normally a person just illuminates the immediate area around her. The more spiritually advanced the individual, the greater the amount of light that is brought into the world, and the larger the area of influence. A spiritual group also radiates light. It is a point of light in space that can have a very beneficial effect on its environment.

However, individuals and groups can be trained to work with light consciously. Different individuals have access to different levels or frequencies of light. Some spiritual practitioners work with light entirely on the inner planes, while others work to bring it into the outer world.

Light that is knowingly radiated into the world has a different vibration from light that is unknowingly brought into life. Light that is knowingly directed carries consciousness. It vibrates at a higher frequency and can directly interact with the consciousness of those whom it affects. Light that lacks this frequency of human consciousness can influence consciousness only indirectly. For example, it can create an atmosphere in which we can see ourself more clearly or help us to act in a more beneficial way. It can help to raise the level of awareness. But light that carries consciousness can speak to us directly. Its light can interact with our own light in a dialogue of light.

Certain knowledge can be communicated only with light, and light can allow other knowledge to be more clearly and exactly communicated. When light speaks directly to light there are not the distortions of reflection, in the same way that when individuals communicate from essence to essence there are not the distortions caused by projection or misunderstanding.

We have begun to work with light on a physical level, one example of which is fiber optics. A fiber-optic cable enables long distance communications to be almost instant and undistorted. This points to the potential of light as a medium of communication. Lasers also illustrate the exactness of working with light. But there are other dimensions of light that have their own science, and this knowledge has been the secret of spiritual traditions[2]. As physical science and esoteric knowledge begin to come together, we can learn how light works in the inner and outer worlds and in particular how it affects consciousness.

For the Sufi, real knowledge is light, "light which God throws into the heart of whomsoever He will."[3] Real knowledge has no distortion or misunderstanding. It is absolute rather than relative. The consciousness of light transmits real knowledge. On the plane of the Self, knowledge is directly accessible. Light is given without effort. But how can one bring this light down into manifestation without its losing its ability to communicate real knowledge? How can one work with this light without having its knowledge become distorted through reflection?

In the Sufi tradition light and knowledge are reflected from heart to heart. The heart is the organ of the higher consciousness—the consciousness of the Self. Spiritual teachings can be reflected or impressed directly into the heart, bypassing the limitations of the mind. Because it does not belong to the level of duality but to the oneness of love, this process of reflection has no shadow. In this way the teachings can remain pure and uncompromised. But in order for the teachings to be received, the heart of the recipient needs to have been awakened, to be spinning with the higher frequency of divine love. This is why such teachings can only be given to initiates. If the heart is not awakened, if the eye of the heart is not opened, then nothing can be directly received.

A further part of the Sufi training is to bring the mind into the heart, the mind "hammered into the heart" as the Sufis say, so that the teachings given to the heart can be assimilated into everyday consciousness. A mind that has been brought into the heart can understand the ways of oneness, which are often paradoxical, sometimes even nonsensical, to the rational self.

An initiate is one who has been awakened to oneness while living in the world of duality. But can the light of oneness also be given to those whose hearts have not been awakened, who are still caught in the illusions of duality? Can the knowledge that is transmitted through light be made available in the realm of duality without losing its essential nature?

The crucial moment in the work of bringing light into the world is when it hits the plane of reflection. Without conscious direction, the light then gets split into rays that carry only part of its knowledge. This is like seeing one's reflection in a mirror that is broken into many pieces. There is no true picture, just fragments of truth. Each image is a distortion of the original image. If knowledge is given in this way, it too becomes fragmented: its wholeness is lost.

But there is a way to bring light from the inner planes to the outer world without its essential knowledge being distorted. Openings have been made between the worlds to enable this to happen. These are like corridors of clarity, places where direct perception is possible to people who have not developed this organ of spiritual awareness. In previous eras sacred sites and buildings were designed to make a higher level of awareness more easily accessible. One can still feel this in places like Chartres Cathedral, while a stone circle like Stonehenge holds more distant memories. These sites were not just places of devotion, but also places where esoteric teachings were developed.

For example, Chartres had its own school where music was composed to be played in harmony with the sacred geometry of the cathedral. The music and sacred geometry aligned the individual with his inner body of light, helping his spiritual development. Most of these teachings have been lost.

The web of light and love that has been made around the world is the container for the spiritual teachings of the future. It is global rather than insular, belonging to the whole of humanity rather than to a single culture or place. Working with this web, we can help direct light into the world in its purity; the teachings of oneness can be made accessible not just to the initiate. Knowledge can be given directly to the heart of humanity.

SPEED AND MERGING THE WORLDS

Spiritual evolution has to do with speed. As humanity evolves, it is speeded up. This is reflected in the pace of life in the West, and in the speed of our technological developments.

The inner worlds move faster than the physical world, and it is this difference in vibration that makes spiritual reality difficult to understand. The mind accustomed to the slow pace of normal life literally cannot grasp the faster speed of spiritual teachings. However, as our outer world speeds up, we come closer to the vibration of the inner worlds. Irina Tweedie describes her realization of the importance of speed when she was living in a room in London next to a traffic intersection:

> To my surprise the quick vibrations of the traffic not only did not interfere with meditation states, but proved to be helpful. And the day came while meditating, I began to realize why the Spiritual Life, or Yoga, is a question of speed. He [her teacher, Bhai Sahib] said it himself, I remember, one day. "Life in the world, civilization, is speeded up constantly; everything is going faster and faster. Our children for instance are much faster than us; they live quicker. The pace of life, the pressure of it, the blaring of the radios, the noise of the big cities, does not disturb them, but it disturbs us, because we are much slower. New discoveries, the sciences, inventions, follow each other with hair-

raising acceleration. And the day must come when the Spiritual Life and the life as it is lived in this world are bound to meet; they are like two ends of the same stick; they will meet in the middle and become one."[4]

As the speed of outer life comes to meet the speed of the spiritual dimensions, the light of the inner can flow into the outer. At the moment this is happening at certain places where the energy structure of the planet has optimum potential, where new ideas can come to the surface with the least resistance. Throughout history, specific places have been centers of development. Florence, for example, was the center of the outpouring of energy that was the Italian Renaissance. Today, when the most obvious signs of development are in computing rather than art, Silicon Valley in California has become such a center for technological development.

But the present work is to give the whole of humanity access to a higher awareness, to allow the light to flow beyond those specific centers to the whole planet. Our evolution needs to be global rather than insular. If we are going to work with the light of oneness in the collective consciousness of humanity, we need to know how this light functions in the realm of duality, how it affects ordinary consciousness.

How much reality can our perception bear? Bringing the inner into the outer is a delicate task. The web of light around the world has been designed to help in this work of merging the inner and the outer, to give us access to oneness without danger. This process is being tested at the present time. Because this container is organic and not a fixed pattern, it can easily be adapted and changed. The masters of love are working to see how light can be reflected into the world without losing its essence, without any dilution of the potency that belongs to this purity. They are carefully watching the reactions of human consciousness.

There is always the danger in giving something of such purity to humanity that it will be misused, just as global consciousness is sometimes misused in patterns of corporate greed. When the light of oneness is given, it is given freely and without restrictions. This is part of the nature of this light; its use cannot be conditioned. But it can be given with the knowledge of how it can be used to benefit humanity, and also given in ways that are veiled from those who would misuse it. Love and light have their own subtleties. There is a way to reveal something so that it is only apparent to those who are not caught in the grip of their own desires. If something of great value is given away freely, it rarely attracts the attention of a mind conditioned by greed. A Sufi saying expresses this simple truth: "We stand in the marketplace with our hands full of jewels, saying, 'Take them. They're free.' But people pass by because they think they are false."

This light that is being given to the world is of a high frequency; it comes in just at the borders of consciousness. A mind that is focused on material gain or ego-oriented power will not be able to grasp it or know how to use it. It is moving too fast to be held and is too free to be controlled. And in order to work with this light, one needs to be in the present moment; a mind that is caught in the future or the past cannot see it. Part of the potential of this light is to open the present to the possibilities that belong only to the moment, to help germinate the seeds of an expanded awareness.

The masters of love have worked to tune this light so that it can help change our consciousness, not only on an individual level, but also in the collective. It can help awaken us to the oneness that is around us and to humanity's role as the consciousness of the planet. The light can show us our potential and responsibility, and it also carries the knowledge that we need in order to make this step. Real knowledge is always given from a higher level of awareness. The real understanding of global awareness must come from the plane of the Self, which is a plane of oneness. The Self carries the knowledge we need in order to live this new awareness, a knowledge that is given as a light which is free, unconditioned, and uncontaminated.

In order to consciously connect with this light, to absorb its meaning, we have to turn away from any self-interest, whether physical or spiritual. This light is about the development and meaning of the whole, and is not visible through eyes that are concerned only with the individual. This is one of the simple safeguards against its misuse. However, because our collective attitude is so self-absorbed, it is difficult for the light to penetrate the collective, or for it to be noticed and then used. And yet this light is desperately needed by the collective for our evolution and for our very survival. To bring this light into the collective is a real challenge.

Humanity is being speeded up so that spiritual and worldly life can become united, the two worlds flow together. This is symbolized by the number eight in which the two circles flow together. (Eight is the archetypal number of our coming era.[5]) And yet in the West, where life is already so speeded up, the increased speed appears to be absorbing us more and more in the demands of consumerism and personal gain rather than opening us to a different awareness. People's lives are becoming more hectic in the race for material well-being, more caught in the density of desires. Even as the light of oneness is being brought into this marketplace, our thought-forms insulate us from it.

How can the collective be turned towards what is being given? One of the ancient ways is to give a shock to the collective so that it becomes free of its conditioned attitude. The shock often comes in the form of a natural or man-made disaster. At times of disaster people traditionally turn towards God; they look to the salvation of their soul rather than their material well-being. However, because of the need for a global shift in awareness, such a disaster might have to be global rather than local, and its consequences could be so overwhelming that humanity loses any thread of real awareness. When the fight for collective physical survival is the focus of our attention, we might completely forget the world of grace.

Can we be awakened through love rather than violence, through joy rather than despair? Does a world have to be destroyed in order for humanity to evolve? We have seen so much suffering in our history; so many wars have been fought. Do we need another catastrophe? Can we step into our role as adults with dignity rather than desperation?

Love has its hidden ways, its paths of silence and seduction. Maybe the consciousness of the collective can be subtly shifted so that it can see the dawn that is breaking, the wonder that is being offered. His lovers know that "His mercy is always greater than His justice." He can change the heart of humanity, draw back the curtain of our self-absorption. But we need to ask for divine grace. Our prayers draw down His attention. Standing in the marketplace where we need His light, we call to Him. We ask that what is hidden be made visible. The two worlds are so close together that only a single shaft of sunlight is needed to help us to see.

AN ORGANISM OF LIGHT

There is a way to bring light into the hearts of humanity, bypassing its collective thought-forms. In the heart of every person is a spark of light, the secret of divine presence. This is the seed of our consciousness. Without this light there would be no consciousness. This is also the spark that draws us back to God. If enough mystics come together in the midst of the world, they can use the mirror of their hearts to reflect light directly into the consciousness of the collective. Divine light will speak to the light within the hearts of others. The light of His love can bypass the mind and infuse its knowledge into the collective consciousness.

Permission has been given for this work to be done. Mystics have been working together to form a living organism of light that can work directly with the heart of humanity. Part of the power of this organism is that it is not dependent upon any one person or fixed idea, but is a fluid and amorphous entity that can be present in many places at the same time. It is working to free humanity from the limiting constructs of power as well as from other forces that dominate our collective. It is activating cells of light within the collective, cells that can communicate with each other. The most difficult part in this work is when it begins to become conscious, because then it hits the patterns of resistance, the thought-forms that influence our present collective consciousness. This is when the pure light of direct knowing hits the reflective surface of everyday consciousness.

If the collective cannot accept what is given, the light will simply be reflected back into the empty space of the unmanifest. The knowledge that is in the light will be lost. But if the collective is porous enough, then

the wisdom of oneness can permeate our everyday knowing. We can begin to see life with the eyes of oneness, with the knowledge of how oneness works in the world.

Activating cells of light within the collective can help to break down the surface of resistance from within the collective. This work is urgent and yet it needs to be done with patience; otherwise it could fragment the collective. Too much light too soon could cause our existing collective ideologies to crumble before humanity is ready. The insecurity this would cause would be dangerous, making people revert to tribal or racial patterns that are the antithesis to global unity. There are already hints of this danger in our present world situation. Humanity would then become more insular and fragmented, and more vulnerable to the apparent security offered by structures and relationships based on dominance, the hallmark of hierarchical power structures.

The importance of moving from hierarchical power structures to a living organic structure cannot be over-emphasized. Only a structure that is organic and alive can change and develop with the speed and flexibility needed for the two worlds to merge, for the inner and outer to be united. Any hierarchy would be too brittle to assimilate the fluidity of the inner world. Hierarchical power structures are the dinosaurs of the present time, too slow-moving to adapt quickly to global change. Their centralized systems also consume too much energy and other resources, and they are too entrenched to be open to new modes of energy and awareness. And most important, they do not utilize the potential of the individual as a dynamic center of consciousness. One of the wonders of global communication is the ability of anyone to communicate directly with anyone else. This has both a practical and symbolic meaning, pointing to a new era of interconnectedness and relating that is not supported by hierarchical structures.

Creating an interconnected organism of light is one of the first steps in the foundation of a new global awareness. This organism is formed from our own consciousness linked together with that of others in a way that supports our individuality and nourishes the whole. Its principle is freedom rather than control, and it works with the inherent oneness of life. Its unity and dynamic flexibility will create a container for a new level of human development in which the inner and outer can directly interrelate, the physical and symbolic worlds nourish each other, and the pure consciousness of the Self give us the knowledge we need. This may seem idealistic, but its shadow side will also be present. We will still have to confront our darkness, our failures and weaknesses, and we will also have to recognize the misuse of the new knowledge that is being given. But we will have a more direct access to the light of our own nature.

THE DANGER OF PURE LIGHT

It is one of the laws of manifestation that everything has a positive and negative aspect. The light of the Self, the light of our pure consciousness, can have a negative effect. As its energy hits this plane it has a certain ripple effect. As its energy radiates out, it interacts with the environment, with the density of this dimension. This interaction of one energy level with another creates a vibration; it is like striking a musical note. The note itself remains pure, but it can create harmony or dissonance depending on how it is received. It is in this way that the effect of the light of the Self can be positive or negative.

The vibrational effect of this energy brings things to the surface. The light reveals what is hidden. Not everyone wants his or her shadow to become visible and then to have to take responsibility for what has been in the darkness. This is true on both an individual and a collective level. Is our culture prepared to confront the dark side of its addiction to consumerism, the ecological and human consequences of its actions? Our shopping malls have their dark twin in sweat-shops and slave labor. We use the poverty of others in our pursuit of wealth. And the earth suffers as we look only to our own comfort and success. The energy of pure consciousness brings everything into the light, without regard for our need to stay safe and secure in denial. The global marketplace means global responsibility. As both beauty and terror become more visible, our games of evasion will no longer be effective. How we respond to what is made visible is more important than we realize. If we reject the energy of the Self, it can become very destructive. The ego can not so easily defend itself against its purity and potency.

Part of the quality of the light of the Self is that it does not reflect off the surface of things. It shines into the core, the essence, and so reveals what is under the surface. We are used to walking in shadows. We know how to hide what we do not want to see. We know how to shift the blame and avoid direct responsibility. Our politicians, those who apparently decide our collective destiny, are masters of this art. Theirs is a game of "smoke and mirrors," and we no longer expect them to be truthful or honest. Nor is simple, direct truth in our corporate dictionaries. We have become used to a language of deceit and manipulation. This works well in a world of shadows, allowing us to see only what we want. Direct truth is much more dangerous and demanding. It requires that we take real responsibility for our actions and ourselves.

What happens when we can no longer shift the blame, no longer hide in our image of righteousness? What happens when we are confronted by real powers of darkness? This demands an integrity we are unfamiliar with. As darkness becomes visible, we cannot pretend that we are innocent. Only when darkness is directly confronted by truth is it no longer a threat—nothing is more powerful than the light of pure consciousness, the divine light of truth. But in collective patterns of deceit and denial the darkness ferments and grows.

When we deny the light of the Self and the responsibilities of oneness, its energy stays unintegrated. On an individual level this can create imbalance. We try to escape its intrusive light, but our normal patterns of defense do not work. Sometimes this can lead to a personal breakdown, when we can no longer function in denial. What might happen on a global scale when the container of our collective consciousness becomes too fragile? When the safety of our normal existence is threatened by forces we neither accept nor understand? Evolution is a dangerous and painful process.

Working with the light of the Self, we have access to direct perception rather than reflection. We can see things as they really are. The danger of this light comes from our denial, from turning away from the truth. If we continue in our present state of denial, we will be unable to confront the powers of darkness that the light brings to the surface. This darkness will have a global dynamic, and it cannot be contained by an approach that is not global, that does not care for the well-being of the whole. We can no longer afford to project our problems onto others or to be concerned only for our insular safety.

To work with the light of direct truth requires integrity and real responsibility. But it also brings with it a quality of joy that cannot be found in the shadows.

This light can awaken life to its true nature, not some distorted image of our projection. The light of consciousness requires our presence, our participation, our awareness and attention. If we try to shift the burden of responsibility, or hide, we will constellate a negative, destructive dynamic. And we can no longer escape the reality that our actions have a global effect. We cannot hide in an insular identity. This is one of the effects of global communication, the internet, satellite television. Because the Self is our wholeness, when it manifests in the world it is automatically global. The light, the awareness that it brings, is global.

Would it be safer to remain in the past, when the light of the Self was only given individually to initiates? Would it be safer to keep the ways of oneness hidden? The need of the time is too pressing; there are problems that require an input of energy that can only come from a higher dimension. The soul of the world has cried out and the light of oneness is already flowing into the world. It brings with it new responsibilities that are no longer to be carried solely by the masters of love, but belong to the whole of humanity. How we work with this energy will determine our future. The energy comes into life through the consciousness of humanity. Our attitude and attention create the patterns through which it will flow. In our collective consciousness these patterns of the future are coming into being. We are the connection between the two worlds, between the spiritual and worldly dimension. How this connection functions will affect the frequency of love and light that can be directly given from the inner to the outer. An attitude that is open to change and prepared to take global responsibility can carry a frequency that is higher than a consciousness caught in self-interest.

The masters of love are allowed to help, but not to interfere. They can point out the direction, the signs that we should follow. And yet in this world of charlatans and soothsayers it is difficult to know what signs are real. This belongs to the test of the present. In the clear light of the Self the signs are obvious; the teachings are simple. In the distorted images of the ego there are many different paths, each offering its fragmented version of the truth. The new age has its own dangers, its patterns of deception. But when there is joy in the heart, and laughter, the doorway is already open. In the light of the Self everything is a reflection of the Real—if we know how to look.

$\mathcal{P}$OWERS *of* $\mathcal{D}$ARKNESS

And to whomsoever God assigns no light, no light has he.

Qur'an 24:40

DIMENSIONS OF DARKNESS

The realms of existence and nonexistence include different dimensions of darkness. In the realm of nonexistence is the darkness of the uncreated, which is actually pure, undifferentiated light. Analogous to the darkness of outer space, the uncreated only seems dark because of the absence of matter; there is nothing to reflect the light that is present. This dazzling darkness of nonbeing is the home of the mystic, the one who has passed from presence to absence, who has experienced the unknowable emptiness. This is the luminous black light of the *deus absconditus*, the divine self-in-itself.[1]

The darkness with which we are most familiar is the darkness of shadows caused by matter, which hides us from light. Our night is caused by the physical mass of our planet being turned away from the sun, but even in daylight matter hides us from the bright clarity of sunlight. Ours is a world of half-light, shadows, and darkness. We rarely see with the clarity of direct perception. This is as true in the dimension of consciousness as it is in the outer physical world. We do not recognize the true meaning of things, and we do not know our own essence.

Our own darkness is most often that of ignorance. Veiled from the light of real knowing, we struggle to understand and to act. The more clearly we can see, the more we can understand and act in accordance with our real nature. But so often we act in the darkness of our ignorance, in relation only to our desires and conditioning. If the thief saw clearly the effect of his actions, would he steal? If he saw how each act envelops him more fully in darkness, would he continue? If we saw how our cruelty or acts of selfishness affected not only others but ourself, how they poison our own life, would we still engage in them? If we knew how our greed pollutes us, denies us the music of our soul, why would we persist? Our ignorance keeps us imprisoned in the cycles of darkness.

Real clarity can only come from the consciousness of the higher Self, a light that does not cast shadows. But without access to this light, we have developed substitutes; we are like people denied sunlight who make do with candlelight. We prescribe morality instead of acting from a real knowing of right and wrong. In the West we have also developed rationalism as a substitute for wisdom. We think we see clearly with analysis and logic, but analysis and logic offer only shadowy outlines. The danger comes when we mistake these outlines for a true picture. Deep within we know that there is another way of seeing, but the institutions of our world only tell us how to read the shadows. They have written volumes of interpretations, which we mistake for the real fabric of civilization.

We are familiar with the darkness of ignorance, and our codes and customs educate us in its ways. But in the midst of our world of shadows there is a deeper darkness where there is no light, not even a reflection. These are the real powers of darkness, which are not born of ignorance or unknowing. Just as we have forgotten the real light, so have we forgotten this deeper darkness. But as we are given access to the true light of the Self, it will reveal the true darkness that exists. These forces of darkness are absolute. They are not part of the world of duality. They are necessary in the functioning of our world, and of the universe. We need to respect them, and some of us may learn to work with them.

IMPRINTS OF DARKNESS

The darkness of ignorance can be transformed. Through spiritual practice and inner work we begin to access our inner light and free ourselves from some of the shadows that veil us. In the words of Ibn 'Arabî, the light of knowledge "dispels the darkness of ignorance from the soul."[2] We can cleanse the darkness of our misconceptions, gain compassion and understanding. We can recognize the effects of our actions and see more deeply into the heart of things.

On the inner journey we are confronted by the darkness of what has been repressed and rejected, the shadow side of our psyche. Through awareness and love we can integrate our dark side and release its energy. Violence, aggression, sexuality—the powers of the instinctual world can be accepted and transformed. As our consciousness expands, we come to acknowledge the need for these energies; we understand how they belong to our natural self and have a role to play in our lives. Often we find creativity, personal power, and other beneficial forces that have been hidden in the shadows.

Through this inner work we clean the room of our psyche, creating an inner space that can receive the light of the Self. We gain more access to our instinctual nature and a greater sense of our wholeness. In alchemical symbolism, we are turning lead into gold, releasing the energy hidden in the depths. This work of transforming the darkness of our psyche is an important stage on the journey. It leads to an awareness of our collective shadow, to that which has been denied by our whole culture. As we work in the depths, we are able to redeem what has been abused and rejected, and not only take responsibility for our personal well-being but make a real contribution to the whole. These steps are necessary to the evolution of consciousness.

But the real powers of darkness do not belong to our personal or even our collective psyche. We rarely directly encounter these powers in our journey of self-development. And yet they are always present, influencing us, absorbing our own light.

The powers of darkness are real and they demand our attention. As we step out of the limited horizon of our individual self into the dimensions of light, we will also encounter realities of darkness. We can see the imprint of these forces in the pages of history, in the horrors enacted by humanity. There have been times when forces of light and darkness have appeared to battle upon the world stage, as in the war against Hitler and the Third Reich. Then Europe was covered by a dark cloud in which the light was hardly visible. The advent of collective terrorism carries a similar stamp, a primal disregard for life and an archetypal fervor.

The powers of darkness work through human weakness. Just as light needs the vehicle of our sincerity and steadfastness, darkness uses our prejudices, often racial or religious, to activate the violence that is within us. We can see the effects of darkness through the cycles of despair, ignorance, and hatred it incites in individuals and communities.

Doing battle with the instinctual forces of destruction as they are activated and influenced by darkness exposes us to an even greater danger: the potential for darkness to absorb our light, thereby limiting our access to what is higher. Without our inner light we are more easily caught in the darkness of ignorance and the unconscious, where destructive forces can dominate us. Without any inner light to guide us, we are easily swamped by the undifferentiated and amoral forces of the unconscious that have no real humanity.

If one looks carefully at acts of extreme cruelty or violence, one can see that the light of humanity has actually been lost. This is what we have come to describe as "evil." The absorption of light leads to acts of evil, as the core of light that balances the primal darkness of our personal and collective unconsciousness is taken from us. In this case, light has not just been drowned in violence, cruelty, or religious fanaticism. Rather it has been absorbed—it is no longer present. This is the danger of real darkness, and this is what distinguishes it from the usual circumstances of ignorance or aggression in which our light and understanding are often hidden but never lost. In our world of reflected light there is always the choice between good and bad, light and dark. But just as in the world of pure light there is no duality, no reflection, only the light of His love, the real darkness also takes us beyond our relative realm of duality, of choices. The darkness absorbs our individual light and we lose our free will.

There is always a moment of weakness, of prejudice, bitterness, anger, even pettiness, that allows this to happen. One surrenders one's individual responsibility, one's innate knowledge of good and bad. But to be caught in the vortex of darkness that we call evil is very different from the normal conflicts that demand our attention and discrimination. Most people rarely encounter this darkness.

Evil is one effect of darkness on human consciousness, but evil is not the fundamental purpose of this energy. Darkness itself just *is*. While the darkness of our personal and collective psyche can be transformed, we cannot integrate or transmute the powers of real darkness. They originate in a different dimension and follow different laws.

As humanity begins to awaken into an expanded consciousness of oneness and to take responsibility for the whole of life, we will begin to have access to the ways of darkness. We will learn to differentiate between the effects of ignorance and the effect of the absorption of light. And we will learn to work with real darkness as a force in the universe that requires our attention and our respect, in ways that come from awareness rather than fear, that do not engage us in conflict or battle.

WORKING WITH DARKNESS

Darkness is a constellation of energy that absorbs light, so it appears to be the opposite of light. But in order to work with darkness we must begin to understand that its nature is absolute. Pure darkness exists beyond the realm of duality and the dimension of ordinary consciousness.

Mystical consciousness has long known of the existence of this darkness. As mystics "keep watch on the world and for the world," they know the influence it has on the world. Their work of witnessing is a detached awareness, combined with compassion for the effects of darkness. But although the darkness causes so much suffering, once one has seen its real nature one has a deep respect and awe, recognizing in it the imprint of the Absolute.

Pure darkness requires respect; otherwise we will remain its victim. We have realized this in our interaction with the unconscious, whose demons require respect if we are not to be dominated by them—it is dangerous to dismiss the monsters of the deep, the dragons of the inner world. Accepting the divinity of darkness, we do not need to turn away from its power, because we stay within the protection of the One who is all. The power of consciously aligning with the divine protects us with His energy.

As the One reveals Itself through creation, the energy of darkness has a role to play. And as the process of revelation changes, so too does the role of darkness. At the beginning of this new era the patterns of revelation are changing.[3] An essential part of this change is the increase in humanity's conscious participation in the process of revelation. This means that the darkness will be present in a new way, one that demands our greater participation. The powers of darkness are to be revealed not just as a reflection in humanity, personified as evil, but closer to their real nature.

Throughout time, individuals have worked with darkness for the sake of our evolution. These masters of darkness are hidden from us, just as the masters of light are veiled. The masters of darkness are working for the evolution of the whole, even though darkness would appear to be a force contrary to evolution.

The masters of darkness have a power that cannot be found in the light. Real power is always an expression of an aspect of the divine, of that which is beyond our understanding. As human beings evolve, we have access to qualities of power that before would have been understood as evil.

Only the mystic who is not frightened of nonexistence can approach the darkness without fear of destruction. One who has been absorbed in love can encounter forces that would damage anything created. Free from the opposition of good and evil, the mystic has passed through the ring of fire that keeps humanity within the sphere of cause and effect. Protected by both the darkness and the light of love, the mystic recognizes that everything belongs to the One. We may have fear or awe before this aspect of the Absolute, but we are surrendered to That which is beyond light and darkness. And there is work to be done with the powers of darkness. There is an energy that is needed to help humanity, an energy that belongs to the dark side of God.

Little is known about the work mystics do for humanity, how often His servants have interceded with forces that would unbalance life, with energies of destruction that flow out of the infinite. They could not do this work if they looked only to the light. They have worked with the forces of darkness since the very beginning. They know their way through the unknowable, through the vast emptiness and into the hidden places where divine light seems absent. They know how to balance the forces of light and darkness within their own hearts, and some have been given knowledge of their chemistry and patterns of interaction.

In the Taoist symbol of yin and yang there is a point of light at the center of the dark circle and a point of darkness in the white circle. This images one of the laws of creation, the need for both darkness and light. The chemistry of their combination is an esoteric secret, but it is important to realize that there is a need for darkness not only on the physical or the psychological level. The expansive forces of life need to be balanced by contraction; radiance needs absorption. Without this balance life would spin into dissolution.

A certain amount of darkness needs to be brought into consciousness for a step in evolution to take place. There is a way to work with the darkness without its being destructive, without its absorbing one's light. The darkness can then become present within life without constellating evil.

A purity of heart and emptiness of intention are needed to do this work. One must be able to access the uncreated dimension of nonbeing. There, one is present in the emptiness of love. Love is the greatest protection when one encounters darkness, because love is not limited. Love does not take sides. Love knows no division. Love is present everywhere, even when it seems to be lost. And love has an energy that fully protects us as long as we want nothing for ourself and are in service to our Beloved.

Love can take us to the places of darkness. In such places it is easier to work from a state of absorption, of absence rather than presence. Some consciousness remains, but it is not a personal or individual consciousness. It is a consciousness without form or substance, without identity.

The energy of darkness draws us back to unconsciousness, to unknowing. But the mystic is familiar with unknowing. She has surrendered herself to the Unknowable. In the depths of her surrender she is held beyond form, and can thus encounter pure darkness without being annihilated by it. Her essence is already absorbed in the emptiness, and this emptiness, which is also the fullness of love, protects her.

DARKNESS BEYOND DUALITY

As we mature from children into adults responsible for our planet, we will be shown more of the forces that influence us. But the revelation of darkness needs to be gradual; otherwise we could be overwhelmed by its presence. Just as light can blind us, darkness can destroy us. We are not familiar with the darkness that absorbs the light, which is why we mistake shadows and ignorance for evil. The existence of real evil has become more of a myth than a reality. Like children, we have been protected from the truth around us.

We can only understand and appreciate the powers of darkness when we step outside of the ego. Beyond the limited perspective of the ego, we can acknowledge the existence of real darkness and see that it is not other than the divine. If we deny the divinity of darkness, we will become its victims. Pure darkness has something else to offer us, which has to do with our place in the cosmos, in the larger dimension of creation.

Darkness is one of the poles of His revelation. Just as in the totality of light, in the totality of darkness there is no recognition; nothing is reflected. Light cannot escape this vortex of darkness. This can be understood as His denial of Himself, divine consciousness hidden from itself. And yet the absolute nature of this darkness is a reflection of His absolute nature. Anything that is absolute can only be a direct expression of Him who is Absolute. That which is absolute belongs only to God.

In our relative world we have created a concept of God that belongs to duality. We are caught in the relativity of light and dark, good and bad, pleasure and pain. We naturally project this dualism onto the divine, whom we regard as good in opposition to that which is bad or evil. As we struggle towards the light, we deny His totality.

But the divine is not an expression of our relative consciousness. We can see this in our constant dilemma about the nature of suffering. How can a God who is good allow suffering? The mystic knows that the absolute nature of the divine is far beyond such seeming contradictions. In the journey towards wholeness we begin to break this conditioning, and this enables us to make the transition towards the reality of oneness, of pure consciousness. The mystic who seeks neither heaven nor hell but only the feet of her Beloved is grounded in a different dimension, one that is absolute and not relative. In Sufism, the *dhikr* "*Lâ ilâha illâ 'llâh*" is a direct expression of His absolute nature in this world of duality. There is no god but God.

Our ordinary consciousness is so conditioned by duality that it can hardly grasp the simplicity of that which is absolute. We look for shadows and reflections, while the dimensions of pure light and pure darkness have neither. Pure light and pure darkness *are not opposites*. This would imply duality, and they do not belong to a realm of duality. When they interact with this world, they are experienced as the primal duality, but this is not their essential nature.

From the perspective of the ego, the power of light and the power of darkness appear to be primal opposites. But the mystic has experienced how the depth of unknowing is also a quality of knowing, how the absence of light and the presence of light can coexist. Pure darkness is terrifying *because it is absolute*. Does this mean that we need to embrace evil? No. Spiritual maturity requires that we acknowledge and accept that there are different levels of reality with different laws, which require different kinds of attitudes and actions.

The mystic lives according to the need of the moment. We may know that everything is One, but everyday life requires that we accept a reality that is relative. In this world, we turn away from the darkness towards the light. This is an expression of the divine imprint within us. Human consciousness aspires to the light and the good. But at the same time we carry the deeper knowing of a reality beyond duality. We know that the thief and the murderer are God as much as the saint. Part of the work of the mystic is to be a link between different levels of consciousness, between duality and oneness. Through this connection the relative world can be nourished directly from the level of the Absolute.

THE PURPOSE OF DARKNESS

Pure darkness belongs to the development of the planet. It is a cosmic energy. Its purpose has to do with the relationship of our planet to the galaxy of which it is a part, to the vaster forces that exist beyond the boundaries of our world. Until now our interaction with these forces has been hidden from us. But humanity's present step towards global responsibility includes becoming aware of certain cosmic forces. Each step of our evolution requires an awareness of more of the forces that interact with us.

The revelations of darkness belong to the absence of light, to a contraction so intense that nothing escapes. There is a power present in this dynamic that belongs to our existence, even as we struggle against its effects. When we perceive this power beyond the limitations of duality, it expresses its essential nature, its quality of the divine. There is a divine darkness, the darkness of the uncreated, that is full of light, but the divine darkness that appears within creation is absent of light. Here contraction, darkness, and power create a black hole of intense force. Astronomy has discovered that at the center of our galaxy there may be a black hole. Is it this which holds the galaxy in place, countering the expansive energy of creation?

In its essential nature, pure darkness is not an absence of light, but a constellation of energy that absorbs light and so appears to be the opposite to light only from the perspective of duality. On the plane of pure darkness there is no duality; light and darkness are just different aspects of the oneness, different potencies of His power. In the words of a Mandean text, "Light and darkness are brothers, emanating from the one Mystery."[4] Pure darkness, like pure light, has a purpose beyond our ordinary knowing.

All is One. In darkness the One is also present. Absorbing rather than radiating light, darkness draws everything back to darkness, like a black hole that draws matter and light into a point of unimaginably intense density. The density of darkness is as important as the expansiveness of light in the process of evolution. Without this density life would lose its balance. Divine revelation could then not take place.

The work of the mystic is to help create a container for darkness that can enable humanity eventually to work with its energy without being destroyed. The web of light and love that is being woven around the world by the souls of the servants of God is a container for both light and darkness. Because this work is being done from the level of the soul, it does not belong to duality. It can embrace and contain light and darkness not as opposites, but as aspects of the divine. Only when these energies are contained in a way that does not constellate opposition can the higher potential of their two natures be realized. We know this within our own personal development: the way the darkness of the unconscious can be combined with the light of consciousness to reveal our own wholeness. How this works on a global scale is different, and yet it is similar: the combination of light and darkness can lead humanity to an awareness of a cosmic wholeness.

The web around the world has a purpose relating to our future evolution. It can be seen from space as an organism of light and love. But it needs darkness in order to have substance and to function on a certain frequency. The presence of darkness gives it a density and also a quality of direction. Through darkness the light can be directed rather than simply radiating in all directions.

A light-source naturally radiates its light in all directions. The ability of pure darkness to attract light enables the light to be focused in a particular direction or directions. The focusing of light is similar to the focusing of consciousness that happens through our attention.

Directed consciousness has far greater potential than diffuse awareness. The ability to focus our awareness is an important step in development. For the individual it begins with the acquisition of language, the *logos* principle. Through the acquisition of language the diffuse awareness of an infant becomes differentiated as objects and people take definite form. Language then enables a degree of interaction and communication that is impossible with only a diffuse awareness.

Through the interaction of light and darkness the energy that radiates from our planet—the light that is in part the collective consciousness of humanity—can have substance and direction. What does this mean on a global level? Focusing and redirecting the collective consciousness of humanity would enable us to interact and communicate with forces beyond our planet. It would allow us to consciously take our place within the larger framework of our galaxy.

The dazzling darkness is full of light. The pure darkness has a different substance, an intense density that is also part of God's hidden purpose. It contains the mystery of how He sacrifices something in order to reveal Himself. Traditionally the darkness belongs to the demiurge, the cosmic force behind the world of matter, which in Christianity became associated with the devil.[5] Our soul's immersion in the world of matter seems to hide us from the pure light of the Self, but without the density of matter there can be no knowing; light would have nothing to reflect off of. Without reflection, all the colors of creation would remain hidden.

Awareness of the real nature of darkness is related to an understanding of the nature and possibilities of matter. The science of the future will explore the ways that matter both absorbs and reflects light. We will come to know that there is an energy, a quality of consciousness, hidden in matter that is waiting to be set free. Our perspective of duality, in which light and darkness, consciousness and matter are separate, will give way to an understanding of oneness that can penetrate the deeper secrets of life and the universe.

Humanity as a whole is not yet ready to work with the powers of darkness. This requires a further step in our evolution. But humanity does need to recognize the existence of darkness, and to know that it is not a force working against our evolution. It is part of a greater pattern than we are presently aware of. It belongs to the evolution of the planet. We need to know that the forces of darkness are not in opposition to the energies of light. That is just how it appears on the level of individual consciousness. Spiritual maturity always requires that we acknowledge a reality beyond our comprehension.

The light needs the darkness. Through the darkness His mystery becomes visible. The powers of darkness express themselves in the world of creation, in the substance of matter, but they do not originate in this dimension. The alchemists understood the demiurge as being present in matter and also holding a magical key that could unlock the closed doors of matter.[6] The unlocking of matter can be associated with freeing, or awakening, the world soul, the *anima mundi*. In our individual journey of awakening we come to experience how the physical world is no longer a place of imprisonment for the soul, but a place for us to realize and enact our true nature. The awakening of the soul of the world can allow humanity as a whole to begin to realize and enact its larger destiny. We can consciously participate in the vast unfolding of love that is happening throughout our galaxy and beyond.

REEDOM

The thief
Left it behind—
The moon at the window.

Ryôkan[1]

THE LIGHT OF FREEDOM

Most of us associate freedom with choice and with being able to do what we want. This common understanding of freedom belongs to the ego, and it often imprisons us more fully in the cycles of our own desire. In the dimensions of light, freedom is a vibration of the soul. The freedom of the soul is not expressed through action; rather it is a quality of being. Different souls express this quality to greater and lesser degrees.

Much of the work of the mystic is to bring the beneficial inner qualities of the soul into the outer world. Because we have associated freedom with the ego's desire to choose, we have lost its vibration, lost our access to its specific frequency of light. For our evolution, we need to know freedom in its essence. We need the vibration of light that belongs to freedom.

The light of freedom can release us from the grip of desire that is bleeding our planet. Our association of freedom with material desires has fed the forces of consumption, forces that are now dominating our planet and threatening its ecosystems. The light of real freedom can activate circuits in the brain that can free us from the illusion that success in life means having what we want. This light can open us to a different way of relating to life, and thus allow life to respond in ways that are not conditioned by our self-centered attitude. Because life mirrors our consciousness, our attitude towards life determines much of life's behavior, how it interacts with us. The freedom of the soul can free the energy patterns of life and allow life to respond in ways it can not at present.

As mystics, we know that life gives us what we need on all levels. We also know that what we need is often different from what we want. We have surrendered our desires to the greater needs of love, and this surrender gives us access to real freedom. Our attitude of service is a direct expression of our freedom—as the Sufis say, "Only the bondsmen are free."

We work in service to love with an attitude born of the freedom of our surrender. We give ourself freely to God and aspire to live His freedom with each and every breath. This is very different from the collective attitude to freedom in our Western cultures. That attitude equates freedom with doing what we want and often rests on a denial of the consequences of our actions; it allows us, like children, not to take full responsibility for our choices and actions. Only too often, as a result, our freedom imposes itself upon our neighbors and our environment.

Our collective understanding of freedom is conditioned by the ego's drama of choice and imposition. We choose what we want, and then impose our will on others and our environment to ensure that our desires are satisfied. But real freedom is beyond duality and so is not associated with choice. And real freedom can never impose itself, because it respects the integrity of all life.

The whole of life knows this freedom—the freedom of creation, the wonder of multiplicity, the diversity of forms, the way "He never reveals Himself in the same form twice." Life is an abundance of wonder and joy. But our collective attitude towards freedom is destroying the multiplicity of life as we pollute our planet to fulfill our desires. From an ecological perspective our freedom is life-denying. From the perspective of the soul, our obsession with fulfilling our desires denies us the deeper freedom that belongs to our divine nature.

THE MATRIX OF CREATION

How can we offer the collective a different understanding of freedom, a freedom that does not impose itself on others or the environment? In the past, humanity has introduced spiritual ideas with the sword, imposing its beliefs in the name of freedom from idolatry or sin. Today we impose our "freedoms" in more subtle ways, for example through our culture's machinery of desire, its patterns of advertising and consumption, and through entrenched elements of our political and legal systems; yet the element of coercion is just as present. Freedom and coercion seem to go together, as if we cannot escape this marriage of opposites. One can see this relationship played out in the United States, in which more people are imprisoned per capita than in almost any other country, despite its advocacy of freedom.

Inner freedom, the real freedom from the grip of the ego and its illusions, is realized through discipline and devotion. It is "that disciplined man," the *Bhagavad Gita* tells us, who "with joy and light within becomes one with God and reaches the freedom that is God."[2] The freedom from the illusions of the ego is often won through an inner battle, known in Sufism as the "greater *jihad*," the battle with the *nafs*, our lower nature.

Yet the deepest freedom comes from surrender, from giving up. This freedom, which is freedom in its essential nature, is never won, but given. It is always present, beneath the veils of the ego, but it is given only when we are ready to accept it. In those veils are woven the things we consider most precious, and we must first be willing to surrender those, too, in order to accept the gift.

The world needs this gift of freedom, particularly at this time of transition. We need to bring this vibration of the soul into the life of the world. Mystics, with the new quality of consciousness that is now being made available to the world, can help in this task through learning to work with the matrix of creation.

Energy fields are the matrix of all existence. All of creation arises from an energy field that exists on the inner planes. This is the matrix of creation, which determines the ways of manifestation. Our culture is so focused on the external physical plane that we have forgotten how creation comes from the inner planes. Shamans and healers have long known how the physical is determined by inner energy fields; healing work often involves purifying an individual's energy field so that the life force can flow freely to heal the physical body. But as a culture, we have never embraced this understanding, and we understand even less about how energy fields work on a collective level.

In the matrix of creation, the energy that flows from the source interacts with the energy generated by life's outer forms. The thought-forms of humanity have a powerful effect on the field. Thought-forms are streams of energy directed by human consciousness. They do not just disappear once they have been thought; they build up patterns that influence the way the energy of life can flow. The thought-forms of our collective conditioning can pollute the creative matrix, limiting the way new forms can come into being. This is one reason why so much attention in spiritual practice is given to controlling and emptying the mind. An empty mind not only enables us to hear the voice of the Self, it also gives us access to inner energy that is not polluted or conditioned. This enables the mystic to live and work outside of the influence of the collective.

Collective thought-forms coalesce and become rigid, forming inert structures on the inner plane that determine the amount and type of energy the collective can access. They sit in the inner world and gather debris, directing the energy flow into constricted but powerful channels, limiting its possibilities while pulling human thought and behavior into its current. Collective or racial shadow dynamics have a particularly strong current, influencing people with prejudices they would not otherwise be susceptible to. Other thought patterns direct our attention down well-worn paths, keeping us caught in old traditions and habits. We need to realize the ways these patterns can undermine our creativity, both individually and collectively. As an obvious example, our Western emphasis on profit kills many creative possibilities because they do not lead to personal gain.

This is where the gift of freedom is so important. The higher energy of freedom can break up these denser thought-forms. It is a spinning vortex of light that can clean away the rigid structures that block the energy field, creating a space where the energy of creation can flow freely from the source. It can give us access to a creative potential that is not influenced by the collective, not determined by the attitudes of the past. But how do we infuse freedom into the matrix of creation?

For the lover of God, real freedom belongs to love. What can be more free than love? Love can not be stolen or imprisoned, imposed or controlled. One cannot dominate with love, because love comes through giving oneself. Real freedom is its essential nature.

Those who have paid the blood money of lovers know this. They know that even in the hunger for love, the darkest nights of love's seeming absence, they are free, because the desire within love is not to possess something—the Beloved can never be possessed. Rather, the desire is to give themselves more fully to love. Lovers of God long to become empty of everything but love, to become nothing, to merge into their Beloved. In the chains of love, that remorseless longing that breaks our hearts again and again, we lose ourself, and love sets us free. This is the real freedom, beyond the ego and its power drives, beyond all the patterns of control and domination that subtly permeate our consciousness, beyond all conditions.

It is through love with its essential quality of freedom that freedom can be infused into the world. Since it is too fine to be caught in the net of conditioning, love can work around our collective patterns, untangling the knots of our collective conditioning just as it works on our personal conditioning, breaking up dense patterns that have grown up over centuries. A consciousness that is attuned to love can reflect the meaning of freedom directly into the core of the collective. It can awaken an awareness of freedom that does not belong to desire or to the duality of choice. Love's freedom flows where it is directed and brings with it a remembrance of the dimension of the soul where we *are free*. This is not an ideology but a state of being.

If this quality of freedom is present in the collective, it can allow many things to happen. Real freedom is a dynamic energy of pure light; when it is present, life is not chained to the duality of cause and effect or past or future; things are allowed to manifest in their essential nature.

There is a danger to bringing freedom into the world, however. The density of collective thought-forms also stops certain negative energy from interacting with us too directly. In limiting the sunlight, we also shield ourself from the darkness. Freedom and anarchy have similar qualities on the plane of manifestation, and in bringing freedom into the world, we expose ourself to the risk of anarchy. This requires of us a much greater degree of responsibility, responsibility of a new kind that relates to the need of the moment rather than the established ways of the past. Creating access to freedom is a dangerous step. If we are to have access to energy that is not determined by the patterns of our collective conditioning, we need to embrace this greater responsibility.

GLOBAL FREEDOM AND THE CORPORATE CULTURE

The presence of love at the core of creation means that freedom is a central dynamic of creation. Creation mirrors the Creator, and He is free. Humanity, made in the image of God, has the potential to live this freedom.

What does it mean to be free? From the beginning of time, freedom and consciousness have been linked. Humanity has been given free will, the ability to make conscious decisions. In Christian myth it was the exercise of our free will, the decision to eat of the tree of knowledge, that banished us from the innocent unconsciousness of the Garden of Eden. On an individual level, too, the movement out of the unconsciousness of childhood is characterized by the development of our capacity to exercise our free will. Each stage in the development of consciousness is accompanied by a development of freedom. Global consciousness will lead us to a greater freedom than we imagine, even as it brings greater responsibility.

We have little concept of what global freedom might mean. We have not yet imagined a freedom in which the freedom of the individual is directly linked to the freedom of the community. But this is the nature of the freedom of the soul: a freedom that belongs to the whole, in which individual freedom never comes at the expense of other beings or of the whole. Our present global structures reflect something quite different. The free-market economy, for example, directly links the idea of freedom with exploitation. Our cheap goods are made in the sweat-shops of other countries. In the name of a free market, we have developed a global system of economic exploitation. Real freedom means the end to such exploitation.

Our present economic structures determine the physical well-being of many millions. It is not necessary to destroy them to end the exploitation that they presently foster, but they will need to be realigned with a global energy that respects the integrity of each individual. Many of us hold a misconception born of greed that if we take others' well-being into consideration it will limit profit and damage business. But respecting the integrity of the individual will release creative potential of each individual, which will work to the benefit of all involved.

Freedom is an important ingredient in this process. Freedom is a part of the divine creative potential within us that is linked to oneness. Its energy reflects a quality of light that comes from oneness, transforming it into creativity and making it available to human beings, allowing each individual to participate creatively in the life of the whole. It is this creative participation that will bring into life the new forms that are needed at this time. Without freedom, the new forms cannot manifest.

Global freedom will necessarily respect all life forms on the planet, because inherent in creation is a balance in which the energy patterns of all aspects of creation are aligned together. God is one and life is an expression of His oneness. This mystical truth is present on a cellular level as well as in the relationship between the forms of creation. But for the energy to flow freely between humanity and the rest of creation, there needs to be a conscious recognition of global freedom, in which the freedom of each serves the freedom of the whole. This freedom, defined not by personal needs or desires but by the oneness of all creation, is not a concept or an ideology, but an inner reality. To become a part of outer life, it needs the participation of our consciousness. It is through us that the inner and outer can unite and be lived as one. We live in a time in which the barriers between the worlds are falling away and a new quality of life is being born, and we are being called to participate in the birth.

Beneath the surface of our cultural and corporate systems there moves an energy with its own agenda, an energy that does not know the distinctions between countries, that does not follow the well-established pathways of commerce and exploitation. This energy is the life force of the planet. It belongs to all of life even as we try to use it for our personal gain.

We can work directly with this life force. As we realize the interconnections of all life, we can align ourself with the life force of the planet and help it to flow where it is needed. But to participate in this work we need to be free, free of personal desires to use this energy and of any preconception of how it might work. The future is being born from a place of freedom and our freedom is needed to bring it into being.

This work is about life in its essence, life that is not controlled or exploited, but *is as it is*. What this means in specific ways we will not know until it comes into being, until it manifests. That is why in order to participate we need to be free of preconceptions. The essence of life resonates with joy and freedom and a simplicity of being, and it is alive with the dynamic energy of creation. This energy carries the blueprint of its own evolution, of the way it needs to manifest. It can bypass many of the corporate constrictions that litter our world, and it can also bypass our own constrictions and restrictions. It follows a different pattern, one that is not caught in the past. Its energy vibrates at a frequency unaffected by present ideologies. It can even bypass our present limited view of freedom. It is alive in a different way.

This creative energy of life with its inherent freedom is already at work in the world. It is bringing new concepts and creative ideas into the marketplace. It is also aligning individuals and groups. It does not have a fixed agenda except the revitalization of life on this planet. It is fighting for the survival of the planet, in direct opposition to the forces that want to control life. It is a living energy that comes into life according to the need of the moment. Often it comes unnoticed, too dynamic and free to be contained in any existing structure, springing up like weeds breaking through the cracks in the concrete. It belongs to the organic evolution of the whole of life, and is a very dangerous force because it does not follow any prescribed pattern. It can not be prescribed, because it is an entirely natural force. It can be aligned, but it cannot be controlled.

The energy itself contains the information we need to understand how to work with it. It just requires our consciousness. Human beings working consciously with this energy can help align it with its highest purpose and allow it to work most efficiently, bringing into manifestation forms that most directly reflect and serve its purpose.

Part of the potency of this energy is its simplicity. But our Western culture and collective consciousness value complexity and sophistication over simplicity. As our thought-forms become more and more complex, we find it difficult to assimilate a relationship to life that is simple and direct. Simplicity is especially not a part of today's corporate environment. And yet corporate structures hold the potential to manifest and implement the global consciousness that is needed now. It is in the corporate world that the value of simplicity most needs to be reestablished, there that the energy of new life needs to flow.

We cannot opt out of our present material culture. Material goods need to flow around the world, and we have the systems in place to facilitate that movement. There is no reason that they cannot work with the energy that flows from the core of life and embraces all of life. Why should we exclude our corporate structures from that flow of energy, when many already have the global reach necessary to implement the flow on a material level?

The internet provides an image of how the energy of life can flow within a manifest structure. The internet is a network that functions highly efficiently and is not delineated by borders or controlled by individuals. It can enable goods and information to be easily accessed, and it allows for an almost infinite array of possible human interconnections which can constantly recon-figure themselves as the need dictates. It is both an organically evolving structure and a part of our market economy. And it is free. In the internet we have been given a blueprint for the future whose full potential we have not grasped because we see it with the eyes of the past. The internet is a direct expression of the emerging energy structure of the planet in which the need of the individual can be met within the organic evolution of the whole, and the evolution of the whole served through the free participation of each individual. It is a model for how future corporate structures could work with the energy of life and embody the freedom that is inherent in it.

FREEDOM AND THE ENERGY OF MATTER

Without freedom there can be no life, no direct expres-sion of That which is free. And yet the denial of freedom appears to be part of human experience at its most fun-damental level. The world of matter seems to constrict us, as the infinite nature of the soul is embodied in the limited world of forms. The dimension of light upon light is inaccessible to our human eyes. And so we long for a freedom that the soul remembers. For centuries spiritual seekers have tried to escape the limitations of this physical world and reach an inner state of pure freedom. Many have made this journey and experienced a reality that is not constricted by space or time. They have seen beyond the horizons of this world, expanded into the inner dimensions of the soul. And then they have felt the pain of returning to the outer world where the limitations of the body and of matter can feel like a prison after the experience of the soul's freedom.

But if one is attached to freedom, how can one be free? If gaining freedom means rejecting something, how can it be real? Freedom is a state of being that belongs to the soul—why should the soul be denied its freedom in this world? If everything is God, then everything reflects His essential freedom. It is always our perception that veils us from experiencing His reality wherever we are.

The world of matter contains a freedom that is a direct reflection of God's freedom. This can be seen in how He expresses Himself in the wondrous multiplicity of forms, in the way no two snowflakes are alike and each moment is different. Life follows its prescribed course; the birds fly south in the winter, and yet each moment is unique, never to be repeated. The constantly changing creation has a quality of freedom that is infinite. In order to experience this freedom of creation, in order to realize that we are a part of it, we only need to change our perception.

When we see the physical world with the eyes of our desires, we experience constriction. In a world of duality we struggle to have what we want, often encountering the pain of denial. But if we approach life with the eyes of oneness, a different dynamic takes place. If we recognize the unlimited nature of life, we step into the freedom of the soul while in the physical world. While we might feel denied what we want, we can still see abundance everywhere around us. The lover knows how the Beloved comes to us in so many ways, rarely in the ways we expect. He who is always with us appears in many guises, sometimes in hunger and in pain, sometimes in love or warmth. If we can recognize His freedom in this world and know that we are a part of His unfolding wholeness, we experience life very differently.

Our spiritual conditioning has set the soul in opposition to matter. But this is a conditioning of a past era. If we can free ourself from this attitude, we can realize the *sacred relationship* between the soul and matter, how they need each other to reveal His oneness more fully. But this means that we have to leave behind the attitude that the world of matter is here to answer our needs and fulfill our desires. We need food, clothing, shelter, but as other cultures have recognized, our needs are met when we live in a sacred relationship with all creation. Life will always give us what we need, even if it comes in the guise of hunger or pain. But we have to leave behind our present pattern of imposing ourself on the physical world. In the words of Hafiz,

> We have not come here to take prisoners
> But to surrender ever more deeply
> To freedom and joy.[3]

It is through our attitude that life comes to us. Making the physical world a prisoner of our need, we imprison ourselves even more than we are aware.

Every cell of creation is stamped with His name and embodies the light of His love. In the midst of matter there is a light that is free. When this light is released, we can have a direct experience of real freedom while in the world. Our collective dismissal of the sacredness of matter has denied us this experience. We have sought freedom elsewhere, or seen it only through the mirage of desires, and in so doing we have kept the light that is hidden in matter trapped, and ourselves trapped in the illusion of matter's constriction. If we can release the light within matter, the world can realize its own freedom. It can come to know that it is not a place of constriction, but a spinning organism of light that expresses in infinite variety His infinite nature. Then the knowledge of freedom that is in our heart can be directly reflected into life, and the mystery of light upon light be present in everyday life.

Once we recognize the oneness that belongs to all the world, we can work within the matrix of creation and discover its patterns of relationship. The relationship between consciousness and matter, or between spirit and matter, does not need to be antagonistic, but like all opposites can lead to the birth of something new. The child born of spirit and matter, made of the substance of spirit and the light of matter, is not imprisoned in the world, but expresses the real freedom of creation.

When we realize how we have imprisoned ourself in our attitudes, particularly in our attitude towards the physical world, our innate drive for freedom will express itself. The tragedy of the present time is that we do not even know that we have imprisoned ourself. We have forgotten the real nature of freedom, a freedom that carries the soul's responsibility to all creation. Instead, we are caught in an ideology of ego-centered freedom that is killing our planet.

Life needs freedom in order to express its magic. Because humanity carries the consciousness of the planet, it is our attitude that will determine whether creation can reveal His freedom. We hold the keys that open the doors to the magic of matter, to the dance of light that is hidden in the physical world.

When freedom awakens, all life will start to sing. In this song, all the forms of creation are alive. Life's violence will still be present, along with its beauty, its joy and sadness, the clamor and the silence. All the aspects of creation will flow together, held by the heart of the world, and from the union of spirit and matter, from the harmony of human consciousness and the physical world, a new era will begin.

$\mathcal{P}$EACE

We are always peace.
To get rid of the idea that we are not peace
is all that is required.

Ramana Maharshi[1]

THE GIFT OF PEACE

Peace, like freedom, is a quality of the soul. And like all real spiritual qualities, it is given. Only when something is given freely does it retain its highest nature. In the words of the Sufi master Bhai Sahib, "How can there be effort with Divine things? They are given, infused."[2]

Inner peace is often associated with tranquility or serenity; it suggests harmony and balance, a state of stillness. Sometimes peace is given through presence. In the presence of a spiritual teacher, we can feel this quality that radiates from within. A spiritual teacher can give peace to his disciples. This was one of Christ's promises:

> Peace I leave with you, my peace I give to you: not as the world giveth give I unto you.[3]

Most of us strive for peace, thinking it can be attained. Outwardly we seek peace through the resolution of conflict. Inwardly we seek peace through inner work or spiritual practice. Resolving our inner conflicts, we hope to find peace as the warring factions of our psyche come into balance. Through meditation we aspire to go

beyond the activity of the mind to reach a deeper stillness, the still depths of the ocean in contrast to the often
storm-tossed waves on the surface.

We might achieve some sense of peace through
struggle and effort. But peace that is given has a different
quality because it comes without effort. This peace is
not a resolution of conflict, either outer or inner. It does
not belong to the dimension of struggle, but to the
dimension of the soul.

Because our culture has lost an understanding of
the ways of grace, we identify peace with effort, with
the resolution of struggle. But real peace cannot be
born from conflict because it comes from a dimension
of oneness. In oneness, how can there be conflict? If
there are not two, how can there be resolution? The
reality of oneness gives a very different perspective on
peace.

If there is no conflict to be resolved, no opposing
parties—outer or inner—to be brought into agreement
or harmony, what is the nature of peace? Peace is a quality of pure being, but like many qualities of the soul it is
hidden within us. The peace that Christ left with his
disciples, the peace "not as the world giveth," is in all of
us. It is a part of our essential nature.

Through the grace of the teacher we are given access
to the peace of our own soul. Can peace that traditionally is given from teacher to disciple be given to the
whole of humanity? Can humanity be given access to
the peace that belongs to the soul of the world?

First we need to recognize that there is such peace.
Just as real stillness is not the absence of activity but a
quality of being, peace is not the absence of conflict but
an inner energy that can flow into life. One can feel the
inner peace of the soul in the presence of a spiritual

person. This peace does not mean the denial of conflict. In the realm of opposites there will always be conflict, just as there will always be the primal opposition of light and dark. Conflict is a part of the dynamic of the realm of duality. Without a certain degree of opposition there can be no growth, no evolution. The dance of opposites belongs to life.

The limitation in our understanding of peace comes from our identification with one plane of reality. Human beings are multidimensional, and yet our collective consciousness has focused our attention on the plane of duality. Astrologically this is symbolized by the sign of Pisces, the two fishes, each fish swimming in an opposite direction. The Piscean era has taken us fully into the drama of opposites, heaven and earth, spirit and matter, masculine and feminine. At the end of this era we have been for so long collectively immersed in its paradigm that we cannot conceive of another relationship to life.

A fundamental part of our experience belongs to the plane of duality and its appearance of opposites. We can never escape the duality of night and day, good and bad, feminine and masculine. Sometimes we experience them in opposition or conflict, sometimes as parts of a larger whole. Struggling or resolving conflicts is a basic part of our human experience. Working with opposites helps us to grow towards wholeness. The danger is when we limit ourself to a single perspective, deny ourself access to other planes of reality. Previous eras have always recognized that human beings exist in the midst of many worlds, and the spiritual teachings of our own era point to realities beyond the physical. How can we have access to the peace that this world cannot give?

BEYOND THE OPPOSITES

During the present time of transition, energies that were previously only available to the initiate are being made accessible to the whole. But these energies need to be claimed and brought into consciousness. The awareness of oneness, with its global and ecological implications, is beginning to pervade our collective consciousness. Peace belongs to the essential nature of the Self, which exists on the plane of oneness. The Self, the inner Christ, can give us the gift of peace, peace that is an expression of love, a quality of our divine nature.

We long for peace and yet peace eludes us. Seeking peace through the eyes of duality, we constellate conflict. Seeking peace with the eye of oneness, we awaken to harmony. Like all divine qualities peace is always present. However, our attention, caught in the play of opposites, does not see His peace. When we see life through the eyes of oneness, a different picture emerges, in which most opposites are two sides of the same coin.

The energy of life often appears to come from the interplay of opposites. Positively and negatively charged particles form part of the basis of matter. Their energy field helps create our visible world. On the stage of human relationships the opposing energies of masculine and feminine play out their drama. This interplay, which contains the promise of union, is fundamental to life.

The initiate is one who has seen this play of opposites within herself and knows that they are part of a greater oneness. No longer caught in opposites, the mystic lives with the reality of union. Having tasted this truth, she begins to see His oneness within all of life. The opposites remain, but they no longer appear in conflict. The mystic sees how His face appears through their interplay and begins to sense the peace that is beneath the surface. As in Judaism's *Midrash*,

> Observe how all things borrow from each other: day borrows from night and night from day ... the moon borrows from the stars and the stars borrow from the moon ... the sky borrows from the earth and the earth from the sky.... All God's creatures borrow from the other, yet make peace with one another.[4]

This peace needs to be brought to the surface. Humanity is now capable of creating conflicts that can destroy the planet. Small groups of terrorists can constellate global chaos. The energy dynamic of the planet has shifted, making more energy accessible to the individual. There is more volatility on a global scale. And yet we remain within the old paradigm, seeking peace through the opposites rather than through the presence of oneness.

The danger of seeking peace through the opposites is that it keeps us on the level of the conflict. Focusing on the opposites can have the increased danger of giving emphasis to the differences. Wisdom recognizes that deep conflicts can only be resolved on a higher level than the conflict. A higher level of consciousness is now being made available to humanity, but we need to claim it. We need to step outside of the security of our polarized vision into the oneness that is all around us. With this oneness we will find the real energy of peace, a peace that belongs to God, to our own divine nature. It is given and not imposed by force.

THE HARMONY OF LIFE

How can we learn to work with the energy of oneness that contains the peace our world needs? How can we be open to a way of being that is beyond our rational understanding, that does not belong to the dimension of duality? In our search to resolve our problems we often overlook the simplest realities. Life contains a harmony that is part of its deepest nature. One can see this in the petals of a flower, in the swirl of the water in a river, in a flock of geese flying south.

During times of transition it is important to return to what is basic, to what belongs to the core of life. This includes allowing life to teach us, to show us how to be with life in a way that does not continually constellate conflict. Life can reveal to us the flow in the opposites, the way night leads to day, winter to summer. Once we change our attitude to life, once we give up the need to control and dominate, then life can show us how to live.

We do not realize how much we are caught in the dynamic of conflict, how we define our life by the battles we fight: battles in our work, in our relationships, with our environment. Humanity will always have the warrior energy; it is a part of our archetypal nature. But in the era of dualism from which we are emerging, it has dominated the collective. The mythology of fighting appears present in every aspect of our life—work, sports, politics; even spiritual life is sometimes seen as a war against the ego.

Are we so addicted to struggle and its drama of the oppressor and the oppressed that we cannot leave it behind? We have fought so many battles with each other and with nature. Sometimes we even define our life by the battles we fight. We are unaware of how much we are influenced by the energy of conflict and by the archetype of the aggressor. We look to a beneficial or peaceful God because our experience in this world seems so antagonistic. But if we look at life, we can see that there is enough food in the world that our primary needs can be met. It is a sad reality that some countries caught by hunger, like Somalia and Afghanistan, have helped create this situation through war, destroying their own basic sustenance.

The energy of life is inherently self-sustaining. Through the process of evolution we can see how life-forms evolve and develop, some becoming extinct while others flourish. Life continually renews itself, and not only on a physical level. We are a part of life, and its energy flows through our consciousness as well as through our body.

When an attitude to life threatens existence, either the attitude must change or existence is doomed. Our present attitude is life threatening. The energy of life demands that we change our attitude. At the same time it is creating the possibility of a different relationship to life both within our consciousness and deep within our cells. The energy of life is present on different levels within us. But we need to be attentive to the changes that are happening all around us, in our hearts, and even within our own bodies. We need to listen to what life is showing us and recognize the ways it is changing and evolving.

A thread is being woven in the inner worlds, but we do not know how to look for it. Harmony is being created out of discord, but we remain focused on discord. The energy patterns of life are subtly shifting; the currents that come from the deep are changing. Life is trying to redeem itself, trying to shake off the debris of our power struggles. And all we can see are the problems that surround us.

THE LIGHT OF PEACE

Peace is born from a place beyond the opposites, where peace is always present. Peace is a dynamic force that we can learn how to use. It has a simplicity that belongs to the energy of the soul. It is a way of being rather than something to be achieved. Once we step outside of the paradigm of the warring opposites, we will find that the sun is shining. We do not need to fight for our living. We have been given the sustenance we need.

The peace is present but we are not using it. In our struggle for peace we create discord: this is one of the effects of working on the level of the opposites. Real peace cannot be imposed, nor is it the result of reconciliation. In our culture of conflict, peace achieved by these means may be the only vestige of peace that is accessible, just as the ego's right to choose is the only concept of freedom our limited understanding allows us. Real peace is a force of life to be lived, to be enjoyed, to be celebrated. It is a gift that belongs to us.

Yet people are frightened of such peace. It cannot be manipulated or attached to power dynamics. In the clash of opposites we fight to win, to impose ourself. Even our image of world peace is a balance of power. What would happen if these power dynamics were removed? How would we know who is in control? The structures of our culture are based upon power dynamics and an adversarial attitude. The drama of power needs adversaries. A life of peace functions in a different way. It does not belong to patterns of control. Peace and freedom belong together.

To be open to peace is to leave behind many of the ways that we define our life. To work with peace would mean that we work with an energy that is free from the constellation of opposites. This energy is a part of our

divine nature. In the Qur'an such an energy is described
in the "verse of Light" from *sura* 24:

> Allah is the Light
> Of the heavens and the earth,
> The parable of His Light
> Is as if there were a Niche
> And within it a Lamp:
> The lamp enclosed in Glass:
> The glass as it were
> A brilliant star:
> Lit from a blessed Tree,
> An Olive, neither of the East
> Nor of the West,
> Whose Oil is well-nigh
> Luminous,
> Though fire scarce touched it:
> Light upon Light!
> Allah doth guide
> Whom He will
> To His Light.

The golden light of the oil of the "Olive, neither of
the East nor of the West" is within us. It is the light of our
divine nature, which is also a part of life. How can our
divine nature be other than the air we breathe? Our breath
is His breath. Through the breath, the soul and the body
unite; heaven and earth are brought together. His light
is "the Light of the heavens and the earth." Behind the
appearance of duality is the light of oneness. We can live
this oneness, this primal union, or we can remain with an
attitude that sees only the continual conflict of opposites.
The light that burns from the oil from the "Olive, neither of the East nor of the West" can show us a different
way to live.

The Light *sura* continues:

(Lit is such a Light)
In houses, which Allah
Hath permitted to be raised
To honour; for the celebration,
In them, of His name:
In them is He glorified
In the mornings and
In the evenings, (again and again),

By men whom neither
Trade nor sale
Can divert from the Remembrance
Of Allah, nor from regular Prayer.

The light that is given belongs to the remembrance of God, the simple awareness of His presence. In this light He is remembered and celebrated, even in the midst of life's activities. We need His light to guide us, and this light is found in our remembrance, our awakening to His continual presence. This means that this light is always available, only hidden by our forgetfulness. The light that is beyond the opposites is not gained through conflict, but comes through prayer and remembrance.

Those who love Him and remember Him have access to the light that the world needs. Our world can never be saved by politicians or mediators, but by those "whom neither trade nor sale can divert from the Remembrance of Allah." The simplicity of this awareness belongs to the core of life, to a creation that celebrates its Creator. Our forgetfulness of Him is what denies us access to this light.

WORKING WITH PEACE

Working with the presence of peace demands an awareness of detail rather than of the big schemes that attract our collective attention. Peace belongs to the simplicity of life, to what is ordinary and thus often overlooked. It is found in what is closest to our natural self. It is here that life is in balance, and from here the energy of peace can be brought into the collective. Once peace is present it can help life to breathe, help to bring the inner and outer together, and at the deepest level allow us to participate in the mystery of *light upon light.*

To restore the balance of life will take time, effort, and devotion. The ravages of the last century have brought life to a dangerous imbalance in the inner as well as in the outer worlds. Many healing, beneficial forces are no longer able to flow into life, and their energy needs to be redirected. An atmosphere of peace in both worlds will enable this to happen more quickly.

But we have become entranced by violence, even using it as entertainment to distract us from the emptiness of our material culture. We have become addicted to the violent thrill, the adrenaline rush. The energy of peace, which is neither aggressive nor confrontational, may seem too passive. It will take time to detoxify this collective condition. Patience is needed to bring us back to an inner and outer balance, and yet our culture does not encourage patience.

The work of bringing real peace into the collective has begun, but it is meeting resistance. Our world contains so many forces that feed off confrontation and foster violence. We have become so used to demanding what we want and imposing our beliefs that we have forgotten how to work *with* life, not against it. But life has a natural rhythm, its own in-breath and out-breath, that we can come to know and work with.

The light of peace follows ancient patterns that flow through our collective psyche. Peace has the patience it needs to work around resistances, to subtly infect our consciousness. And peace has the power that belongs to a dimension beyond duality. Its energy is not scattered or wasted. It does not engage in power dynamics. It works in silence, creating an atmosphere that fosters harmony. Peace can work with the energy of discord, undermining its arguments, changing the flow of energy from confrontation to understanding.

In the 2000 American presidential election a drama unfolded in which the two main candidates won an almost equal number of votes. There was no clear winner. The symbolism was in plain sight: the time of one party winning and one losing was over. But there was no way to bring this into form. The American political system could not function in a manner that was not adversarial. We were caught within the paradigm of the past even though the people had voted for the future. And the deeper irony was that no one seemed to recognize what was happening. As they squabbled over ballot counting they missed the real meaning.

Because the energy on the level of the soul belongs to oneness, it perceives through similarities and underlying unity. It can evoke harmony in ways that are closed to the perceptions of duality. The eye of oneness sees beyond the surface conflicts to a deeper harmony, and can work to bring this harmony into life. And as we recognize the ways of the inner world, we can also work with symbols and archetypes that can free the energy of life so that it can flow without creating discord. Restoring the soul, remembering its reality on a collective as well as personal level, will give us access to many of the tools that we need to restore balance and harmony and to recognize the meanings in the events around us.

But first we need to acknowledge that peace is a power, a force of life. It does not just appear when combatants lay down their arms. If we are to claim our real heritage, we need to recognize such qualities of the soul, and realize that they can have a lasting influence on everyday life. These are the powers that can bring real change, that can alter the way the energy of life flows. Peacemakers are not dreamers but practical people who are engaged with life's substance. At this time they are being networked together, linked by the web of light and love that is around the world and within its psyche. Seeing only the surface events, the daily disasters that attract our attention, we do not notice these inner changes. We do not know about the currents that flow within our collective psyche, how light is being brought to places of darkness, how peace is being made present.

THE ENERGY of MATTER

If the eye of your heart is open
In each atom there will be one hundred secrets.

Attâr[1]

WORKING WITH THE NAME OF GOD

In the center of the world an energy source exists that has not yet been accessible. As the world awakens, this energy will gradually become available, and we will learn how to use it. This energy has to do with the fundamental structure of matter, but it is quite different from atomic energy. Atomic energy is released through splitting the atom, a process of division. It belongs to the end of the era of opposition, of life based upon dualism. The energy sources of the future reflect the dynamics of a new era, based upon synergy and the inherent oneness of life.

We have become used to the constrictions of matter, fought against its limitations, learnt how to fly and talk across the world. Now we can learn how matter is alive and can be awakened. The energy of matter is so great as to appear unlimited. We have glimpsed it through splitting the atom, the dynamics of separation. But the flow of relating, of coming together, can release another form of energy within matter. At its core this has to do with the union of spirit and matter. When human consciousness and the physical world work in harmony, a new era can begin.

Every atom in creation spins freely on its own axis of love. There is no constriction in this motion. The real constriction is the denial of our divinity and the divinity of matter. This denial is what silences the song of the world and closes the door to the light hidden in matter. As the world became identified as a place in which the divine is absent, a solely physical reality divorced from the spiritual realm, we veiled ourself from its magical nature. Influenced by both our attitude and our actions, the world began to die. Our environmental crisis is a direct result of our forgetfulness. It has taken many centuries for our inner attitude to create these physical conditions, but if one is to redeem a situation one needs to return to the core of the problem. Otherwise we are only treating the symptoms.

The physical world needs to be realigned with its own energy source, with the life force that is within it. The quickest way to realign anything is to acknowledge its divine nature. Through the interaction of humanity and life, conscious awareness of God interacts with the unconscious knowing of God that exists within all of creation. Creation can then return to the divine axis that is at its core, and through this axis life will flow in its divine purity, its essential joy. The highest principle can come alive again within creation, and this will release the energy that is hidden in matter. This energy is what is needed to heal and redeem the world.

How do we realign the world? Through the simple practice of prayer and devotion. Through our inner alignment, and through our remembrance of God's presence, light and love flow into the world, awakening matter at the level of its deepest structures. As matter becomes realigned to its divine nature, it begins to vibrate at a higher frequency. It begins to sing, and this song is one of the ways it will heal itself. Song has always been a magical way of healing, and the song of the world has tremendous power. The work of the mystic is to be present as this happens, to witness the awakening of the world. Through our presence we add the ingredient of consciousness, which in its deepest sense is the knowing of His name.

Spiritual traditions have always recognized the importance of the word, the *logos*, through which the first principle, the principle of the divine, can interact through the planes of manifestation while staying true to its essential nature. Through repeating His name, we consciously bring an awareness of the divine into our life, into the world of creation. We help the world remember its own divinity.

The name of God held in the hearts and consciousness of the friends of God is one of the secrets of creation. Shamans and other adepts have always understood how the name holds the magical potential of that which is named. The name of God has been repeated in the hearts and minds of His lovers for centuries. It is carried on every breath, with the flow of the blood and each beat of the heart. Repeating His name with the flow of the breath, we align His name directly with the energy of life as it comes into creation, with the physical outpouring of His love. We consciously give an awareness of the divine principle in life to life.

The name of God has a great power, and when it is said with love and devotion, that power is magnified. Just as the name of God can awaken the divine love within our heart, so can it awaken the divine love within the cells of creation. As the name of God can align us with our divine nature, it can also align the whole of the world with the Unnamable Essence Sufis call Allâh.

In our human relationships, when we say the name of our beloved there is a special sweetness in our voice. When we hold our beloved in our arms and whisper his or her name, there is a special magic to our loving. What is done with our human lover can be done with the heart of the world. We can remind the world that it is loved, that we are all a part of a continual moment of ecstasy, of His love being born into the world again and again.

Our spiritual texts, written during the last era, do not describe how the remembrance of God works within creation. Our spiritual focus has been on the immaterial world, the inner realm of the soul. Volumes have been written on how our inner alignment leads us on our own path back to the Source. But we have lost the wisdom of how the name of God influences the world around us.

Previous eras understood how the many gods were a part of life, and how saying their sacred names could make magic, help the rains to come and the crops to grow. The advent of monotheism replaced the many gods with one God, whose home was in a celestial realm. While religion banished its image of God to heaven, the mystic always experienced His presence within the manifest world, knowing how every atom praises Him. But the mystical science of how His name interacts with life at the level of its fundamental structures—the cells, molecules, and atoms of matter—was hidden. Some minor forms of magic still remained, in which names, symbols, and geometric patterns could influence life. But chanting and sacred songs were used to turn our attention upward towards heaven. The deeper mysteries of how the oneness of life responds to the name of God, and how His name can be used to help the evolution of the planet, remained inaccessible except to those masters who worked within the axis of creation.

THE UNVEILING OF SPIRITUAL KNOWLEDGE

We think of the name of God as aligning us with a God who is within or above us. But in the mystery of oneness there is not the duality of inner and outer, above and below. We are all part of God's interpenetrating presence, and through us His world can be aligned to His divine essence. Through His name His qualities can come into the world more easily, His revelation can make itself known more fully.

This revelation is a continually evolving dynamic process in which we are able to participate more and more consciously. Working with divine energy within creation is one of the ways in which we can work more closely with our Beloved. In the deepest core of the heart, where lover and Beloved are one, His name is our name. Through the heart, and the knowing of the heart, He can bring this oneness into life, this imprint of His essential nature into His world.

We are other than God, for He is beyond even our idea of the beyond. And yet we are also one with our Beloved, because there is nothing other than He. The lover knows these not as opposites, but as part of her paradoxical relationship with her Beloved, part of the mystery of love and service. The knowledge of His otherness protects us from inflation, from the ego's identifying itself with God. The experience of oneness enables us to participate more fully in His revelation, how His oneness is made manifest. Our consciousness of being one with God also enables us to bring His divine essence into the world without the division of duality. This allows the power and majesty of His name, its love and beauty, to work directly with the life of which we are a part.

There is a specific relationship between the fundamental structure of life and God's invisible presence. Divine remembrance can make this relationship known, can make it a part of the consciousness of humanity. Awareness of His presence can remind the atoms of life that they are included in His divine oneness. When the atoms of life remember their own divinity, there is a shift in their frequency, just as there is a shift in the vibration of a human being when she remembers God. This subtle shift in the fundamental structure of life will release some of the energy hidden within matter. Then we will have to learn how to use this energy, how to work with it for the benefit of all life. This will also have a shadow side as people will try to use it for personal and selfish motives. But first it is necessary to bring divine remembrance into the physical world, from which it was banished by the fathers of the patriarchy.

To bring divine remembrance into the physical world requires a commitment to life. For the lover there are a deep joy and fulfillment in being here in this world in service to our Beloved. His name sings in our heart and in our blood. With every step, with every breath, we remember Him, and this remembrance is reflected into life. We bring the remembrance of our true nature from the inner recesses of the heart into the physical world. Through our own practice we begin to see how divine oneness is hidden within creation, and our witnessing of this miracle has an effect upon life. Because we carry the consciousness of life, our awareness of His name awakens the world to its own deepest knowing of its Creator.

In our cultural drive for sophistication we often overlook the simple power of remembrance. We look for complex answers to our problems, forgetting the primal nature of our existence, life's divine essence. Working with this essence, working with the name of God, we can give creation the potency of conscious remembrance. His love can then become alive in a new way; the physical world can turn knowingly upon its axis of love.

The awakening of the world is a science. It is not mystical idealism. Just as the spiritual awakening of a human being follows a careful course, so does this global shift have specific guidelines. We have forgotten the knowledge of how the spiritual and physical dimensions interrelate, how the inner and outer affect each other. For example, there is a specific way to bring the currents of love into matter, just as there is a science in the reflection of light from the inner to the outer. This knowledge is a part of our heritage, and yet it is hidden from us. Ibn 'Arabî expresses this truth:

> God deposited within man knowledge of all things, then prevented him from perceiving what He had deposited within him.... This is one of the divine mysteries which reason denies and considers totally impossible. The nearness of this mystery to those ignorant of it is like God's nearness to His servant, as mentioned in His words, "We are nearer to him than you, but you do not see" (Qur'an 56:85), and His words, "We are nearer to him than his jugular vein" (50:16). In spite of this nearness, the person does not perceive and does not know.... NO ONE KNOWS WHAT IS WITHIN HIMSELF UNTIL IT IS UNVEILED TO HIM INSTANT BY INSTANT."[2]

The unveiling of mystical knowledge is given according to the need of the time. But this unveiling is not performed by a father-figure image of God who acts independent of humanity. Our patriarchal conditioning, in which God is in heaven looking after us isolates us from the participation that is needed to awaken us to the knowledge that is already present. It is through our witnessing and participation in life that a knowledge is made accessible from within us and within life. The organic relationship among all aspects of life is part of this process. Through our participation in life's organic oneness, the esoteric knowledge of how this oneness functions from a spiritual perspective can be made known.

Our work is also to be attentive so that we can recognize this knowledge when it is given. Through the remembrance of the heart we are always attentive. We learn to see the signs of God as they are revealed around and within us. Through our inner and outer attention this knowledge can be given to us and to the world. In the last centuries the knowledge that humanity has been given reflects our focus on the physical plane. We have even developed a religion of physical science. The next stage is to bring together the inner and outer, the physical and spiritual dimensions. The knowledge of how they interrelate, how energy flows from the inner to the outer, is crucial if we are to escape our present imbalance.

REALIGNING THE FUNDAMENTAL STRUCTURE
OF MATTER

Because humanity carries the divine consciousness of the world, it is through us that this spark of divine consciousness can be reconnected to the physical plane. This process belongs to the feminine mystery of creation. Women carry the divine spark within their physical body; otherwise they would not be able to conceive and give birth. Women are closer to the mystery of matter than men are. They experience the wonder of creation within their body. Even if a woman never becomes pregnant she still has this quality in her cells.

Because our patriarchal culture has separated the spiritual and the physical, one of the first steps in healing the planet is to acknowledge the spiritual potential of matter, to align the world with its divine consciousness. Women can do this work more easily than men can. It is a part of their instinctual spiritual nature. This is one of the reasons that in the West more women than men are attracted to spiritual life—there is a work for which they are needed.

Realigning the structure of matter with divine consciousness will take time. There is a resistance to any such fundamental change. Part of the patriarchal power drive has been to deny matter its magical nature; in this way men could gain power over matter. Traditionally it was the priestesses who understood the magic of nature. This developed from woman's innate understanding of the interrelationship of life, how all of life flows together. Men have a deep fear of woman's magical nature and over the centuries many patterns of repression have been imposed to deny her access to her magical power. These patterns also stand in the way of reawakening matter.

Although it is important to acknowledge the existence of these patterns of repression, we should avoid reconstellating masculine and feminine antagonism. It is vital that we step beyond the dynamic of opposition. The new knowledge that is waiting for us belongs to oneness, but it cannot be accessed if we have an attitude of dualism. Our attitude aligns us with the knowledge that is already present. At any time of transition we need to make sure that we are not caught in patterns of past conflicts. However, we need to acknowledge the existence of these conflicts in order to turn away from their attraction, their magnetic pull and quality of familiarity. Otherwise they affect us in the unconscious where we have less resistance. Masculine and feminine antagonism have deep archetypal roots. We can easily be drawn unknowingly into the battles of previous ages.

Although these patterns of conflict exist, the energy of oneness has a greater power. It is waiting to be lived, to be brought into being. It needs to work through us and come into our relationship with life. And because women have a more instinctual knowing of this oneness, they are needed to reestablish certain connections.

We no longer know how matter speaks to us. We have given our natural knowing into the hands of science and technology. Science has been a significant part of our development, giving us a new understanding of life and the physical world. The next step is to marry this masculine approach with the instinctual knowing of the feminine. We need to combine our scientific knowledge of matter with its magical qualities. This will lead to the science of the future.

However, patriarchal scientific knowledge is so ingrained in our culture and so much a part of our establishment that any change will encounter powerful barriers of resistance. Collectively we believe in science rather than prayer. The simple fact that we have forgotten the power of prayer, or placed it solely within the sphere of personal spirituality, shows the degree to which we have isolated ourself from our spiritual nature. We look for rational answers to our problems rather than working with the divine that is our very core.

How can we give space to a new attitude without engaging in conflict? Prayer and devotion include rather than divide. Prayer does not belong to any institution, but is a direct connection to the one power that is the source of every power. The remembrance of God, the repetition of His name, brings His presence into life. Through our prayer and remembrance He can work His magic in His world. He can unveil the knowledge within our hearts, and awaken us to the ways of the future.

A CONSCIOUS STATE OF BEING

The work of the lover is to bring the consciousness of love into the world. This consciousness of love belongs to all of creation, and can be brought into the fundamental structure of life. We carry all levels of creation within us. We also carry within us the blueprint of how all these levels interact. This blueprint is not static, but a constantly changing and evolving process, although it does follow certain laws. These laws are the spiritual guiding principles of humanity and all forms on this planet. They are not separate from creation but are a part of cellular structure and its DNA. It is our ability to read, understand, and enact these laws, these principles of life, that determines the well-being of life and the whole body of the planet. When we transgress these laws, we create an imbalance. It is not that we are punished by a judgmental God, but that we go against the natural way, what Chinese sages called the Tao.

The Tao is life in its essential nature, "the mother of the ten thousand things." Its principles belong to the balance of life:

> The mother principle of ruling holds good for a
>   long time.
> This is called having deep roots and a
>   firm foundation,
> The Tao of long life and eternal vision.[3]

When life loses its harmony we suffer. When we lose our "deep roots and firm foundation" we are easily thrown off balance. As life evolves there are subtle shifts in the way the principles of balance and harmony enact themselves, and part of the work of those committed to spiritual service is to realign life with these shifts. One aspect of this work is done through love. Because love belongs to the core of our being and to all of life, it can flow directly to the heart of matter. Through our participation in life we can bring His love directly into the physical plane, even into the movement of its atoms. Love can be used to realign life, to reconnect life to its natural state of balance and harmony.

This natural state of being belongs to all levels of life. It is not a static state, but evolves according to the shifts in the principles that govern creation. Because our masculine focus is on action and "doing," we look for new ways to act to solve our problems. We overlook the feminine principle of "being" and the need to find a new way to "be." The "doing" capacity has been instilled in us through our parents and so many aspects of our culture. To return to our "deep roots and ... firm foundation" in our natural state of being, we need to translate it into "being" instead.

There is a consciousness to "being" that needs to be included in life, a quality of attention that connects the higher and lower, the inner and outer. We know this attention, this inner state of being, in our meditation and prayer. In inner silence we wait, attentive to what comes from our higher nature. To bring this attitude into our outer, physical life is a challenge, particularly when there is such pressure to act rather than "be." But without this state of conscious being, life will lose its balance; the energy that is coming into creation will not flow into the new channels that have been prepared.

Presence, attention, witnessing are spiritual practices that belong to an awakened state of being. They enable our consciousness to participate directly with the flow of life. Inwardly we are attentive to the principles of life, to the unwritten laws of creation. Outwardly we reflect these principles into manifestation through our attitude and the way we live. This way, the flow of outer life can follow the patterns of change that are happening within. Because we have been so focused on outer action, we have lost the knowledge of how the energy of life can be directed by our attention. A conscious state of being in which the inner and outer are in harmony is a powerful force in the world.

When energy flows freely from the inner to the outer, a new dynamic in life can manifest. The fundamental structure of life will shift in a very subtle way; its axis will change, and this will enable part of its energetic potential to be realized. At the moment, our collective attitude imprisons this energy in matter. This imprisonment is reflected in our present science, which requires that we use force to release the energy in matter in the volatile and dangerous form of nuclear energy.

But when there is a balanced flow between the inner and outer, matter can respond and release its energy freely. Part of this process concerns the dynamic interrelationship of consciousness and energy and matter, which has been suggested by particle physics.[4] Physicists working at the sub-atomic level of matter have noted that the attitude of the observer has a direct effect on the way the energy of matter appears to act. This interface of consciousness and energy will be an important area of future scientific progress. There are ways to work with the energy of matter that are only at the threshold of our awareness, and other ways that at present remain hidden.

Mystics know the ways energy and light can be directed by our attention. Through real attention to daily life we bring awareness and the light of the soul into the outer world. This is described in the Naqshbandi Sufi practice of "Attentiveness," (*nigah dasht*). "Be always mindful of what you are thinking and doing so you may put the imprint of your immortality on every passing incident and instance of your daily life." Also, in our practice of the *dhikr* we can bring the name of God into the world of matter—for example, repeating His name while we cook infuses the food with the energy and love of remembrance. One could taste the love in my teacher's cooking!

Working on the inner planes, through our inner attention, we reflect light and love where it is needed. We can also focus the name of God into the diffuse energy of the uncreated, and use our attention to unblock energy so that it can flow into manifestation.

Other ways to work with the energy of matter will also become available. What we call "magic" is a variety of ways to work with matter on an energetic level, and there are different levels of magic, different ways to work with the energy of creation.[5] This is all a part of the science of how the inner and outer relate. Consciousness and matter are not isolated from each other. When we begin to understand the interdependent oneness of creation and how the different levels of reality are connected, different fields of knowledge will become accessible.

THE ANGER OF THE EARTH

We need to be careful at this time of transition. Matter is not as static or as solid as we perceive. We do not know that the energy within matter can become wrathful, that it can turn against us. In China the earth energy was imaged as dragon, whose power was to be respected. There are forces within the physical world that we do not understand. There are also forces which until now have been dormant, but could easily awaken.

Psychology has shown us that we have unwelcome forces in our personal and collective psyches which can be very destructive when they awake and come to the surface. We know that anger can arise from the feeling of being mistreated or abused, and that this power of vengeance exists on both a personal and collective level. But we have little understanding of how such forces can exist within matter, how its dragon-energy could erupt. We are ignorant and arrogant in our relationship to the physical world. We continue to abuse it without real concern for any consequences.

As the energy patterns in the world begin to change, more energy will flow to the surface. The free flow of energy around the world that we experience in the global marketplace and global communication is an aspect of this shift, but these energetic changes are not happening only on the surface level of business and technology. Something within the core of the world is awakening and making its presence felt. A certain barrier that had defined the physical dimension and held it apart from the energies of the inner world is falling away. This has to do with the merging of the inner and outer, the coming together of these two dimensions.

In our dualistic thinking we forget that a shift in our collective consciousness also means a shift in the earth's energy. Our science may measure the ecological effects of pollution, climate changes, and global warming, but we do not understand the relationship between our consciousness and the earth. We do not realize that there can be a direct energetic relationship between our collective consciousness and the earth's energy patterns.

Responsibility for our planet becomes a central theme as we move into a new era. We need to become more aware of how our attitudes, which are polluting and violating the earth, can disrupt the balance of life. This is not just primitive superstition, but an understanding of the way energy flows in the physical world. In many cultures the work of shamans was to heal any imbalance that we might create in the web of life. To quote Martin Prechtel,

> Shamans are sometimes considered healers or doctors, but really they are people who deal with the tears and holes we create in the net of life, the damage that we all cause in our search for survival.[6]

We may be aware of the danger of earthquakes and climate changes, but we have forgotten that the earth can be angry. We do not have enough shamans to repair any imbalance we have created. We do not know how to work with the energy structure of the world. And these patterns of energy are changing, just as our collective consciousness is shifting.

The heart contains a direct connection to the energy structure of the planet and the ways the energy flows. The heart chakra is the center of the human being, the home of the Self which contains the consciousness of the whole. Because the human being is linked with the whole of creation, the heart gives us access to its energy. The consciousness of the heart can make a real contribution to the balance and flow of the energy of matter. As this energy becomes more awake and active, His lovers are helping to balance it. Like the shamans of previous times, they are working to counter the negative effect of corporate greed and other forces that seek only to exploit the physical world. On a more subtle level they are learning to work with the energy of matter so that its potential can be used beneficially, rather than in the destructive dynamic of chaos.

Until recently, mystics have mainly worked on the inner planes. But the shift in the energy structure of the planet is turning our attention to the physical plane. At the present this work is in its infancy, but the changes that are taking place require careful attention. Through our attention the awakening energy of the world can flow in a beneficial manner, create the river beds that belong to the flow of life in the future.

A MULTIDIMENSIONAL APPROACH

The changes taking place in our world are so new and so profound that we do not have a model in our recent history to help us understand or relate to them. The shifts in the energy structure of the planet are beyond our immediate comprehension. The possibility that the energy of matter could awaken seems pure fantasy. And yet particle physics has prepared us for a paradigm totally different from our present relationship to the physical world. To accept that our consciousness and the world of matter could have a direct interrelationship requires a degree of responsibility we are reluctant to take. But if we do not take this step, the energy that is being awakened could become very destructive.

In past ages mystics and shamans have guided humanity at times of transition. One of the fathers of our Western civilization, the ancient-Greek philosopher Parmenides, was a mystic. Through his connection to the inner worlds he brought justice and law-giving, and laid the foundation for much of our culture. Present Western culture does not honor its mystics, but they are still present among us. Because their work has been primarily on the inner planes, the lack of external recognition has not mattered to them; rather it has enabled them to continue their work without disturbance. But if a certain esoteric knowledge is to be given to humanity, there needs to be a recognition of the tradition of real knowledge and wisdom coming from within.

How do we know what is fantasy and what is truth? The physical world is more strange than it may appear or than we would like to believe. And, as Rumi reminds us, mystics exist in a paradoxical, crazy, reality that is passionately alive:

> Oh daylight arise! Atoms are dancing,
> Souls lost in ecstasy, are dancing....
> They are all like madmen; each atom, happy
> or miserable,
> Is passionate for the Sun of which nothing can
> be said.[7]

Within the heart different worlds coexist, bonded by the oneness of love. The knowledge we need is not separate from us. It is our heritage and also a gift. The earth is alive because everything is alive; "every created atom is articulate with love." Our consciousness does not need to be limited to a reality defined by physical form. It can see what is hidden within matter, know what is hidden within the heart.

But the radical potential of what is being given at this time requires that we step away from our old ways of understanding and perceiving the world. The knowledge of the past has become inadequate. Developments in technology have prepared us for a changing world, one that is more interconnected than we knew even a decade ago. But this is only the beginning of a fundamental realignment that demands our careful attention. The interconnectedness of the inner and outer will take us into a very different world.

We do not understand the physical effects of our collective consciousness. We abuse the earth mentally as well as physically, with no recognition that there could be any consequences. Nor do we understand that the physical pollution of the planet affects us mentally, psychologically, and even spiritually. But once we realize that all of life interrelates not only on a physical level, but across different levels of reality, we will have to embrace a multidimensional awareness.

As this era of masculine dominance comes to an end and a feminine understanding of life's wholeness is included, we are beginning to experience a different world in which physical, mental, and spiritual well-being are interdependent. We see the signs of this in the new age movement. But the new age movement is often limited by its focus on individual well-being. Our real concern is the well-being of the planet and the whole of humanity. Central to this is the understanding that the physical world cannot be healed from a solely physical perspective, but requires a shift to an attitude that contains a multidimensional approach.

Once we make a conscious decision to be open to this vaster, less defined world, life will respond. Life cannot connect with our consciousness until we take this step. The created world has much to teach us, but it needs our conscious cooperation and participation as part of its living organism. If we approach life as separate, we will only see the reflection of our dysfunctionalism. If we approach life from the perspective of oneness, it will reveal the wonder and magic that will help us to heal the wounds we have inflicted upon ourself and our world. The physical world will also teach us how to release the energy it has within it, and how to bring this energy to fruition.

Matter is spinning and dancing with the same love that radiates in our soul. The spinning of the heart and the spinning of atoms belong to the same outpouring of love. The power of love and the energy of matter come from the same source. The web of life is a single outpouring of joy that is becoming conscious in a new way. Life needs us not only to help heal its wounds but to celebrate its awakening. Praise and prayer can align the world with its axis of love, where this celebration has begun.

> Each atom hides beneath its veil
> The soul-amazing beauty of the Beloved's Face.[8]

This beauty is being revealed afresh. If we knew the wonder of this moment, we would become instantly intoxicated. The world may cover us with its appearance of problems, but the love, joy, and wisdom that are being born belong to a different vibration. Through our consciousness this vibration can be infused into matter. Our consciousness can then be linked with the soul of matter and we can work directly with its energy structure. This synergy of consciousness and matter is a gift of our future.

$\mathcal{N}$ONBEING *and* $\mathcal{B}$EING

The moon passes over the ocean of non-being.
In the desire of the One to know Himself
We exist.

Rumi

Is there a real need to understand or participate in the changes that are taking place within us and within our world? The mystical path has traditionally led us to a place of silence and unknowing. Mystics are taken beyond the world of cause and effect, action and reaction. In this place of silence there is neither creation nor destruction; nothing is in balance and nothing is out of balance. Why should we turn away from this place? Why should we reenter the arena of action and participation?

The mystical truth of nonbeing is always fully present. For countless centuries, mystics have carried this truth, immersing themselves beyond any knowledge of self, beyond place or no-place. We may talk about the urgency of our present world situation, of an ecological crisis, but these are just images on the screen of creation. Fundamental nonexistence is not concerned with images on a screen, with comings and goings; it is the deepest, most ancient truth of humanity. Why should the mystic turn her attention back to the images, to this drama of action and reaction? If there is neither cause nor effect, neither action nor self to act, how can there be participation?

There is no answer, because on the level of Truth there can never be a question. When Buddha held up a flower, when al-Hallâj said *"anâ'l-Haqq"* (I am the Absolute Truth), it was not in answer to a question. The relationship between the mystical ground of nonbeing and the world of cause and effect is not easy to describe. But there is a way these two come together, because even to suggest that they are different would be to remain on the level of duality.

The mystic who has passed behind the veils of creation knows that death is just an illusion, destruction just a façade. Who is there to die, what is there to destroy? The mystic who has died before death knows that birth and death are just two sides of one coin. The cry of a new-born child and the last gasp of an old man are the same. The acorn and the tall oak crashing to the ground in a winter storm are not different. Even hunger and plenty, drought and rain, are just the peaks and valleys of the waves of existence. Yet the mystic is present amidst all the mundane activities of life. The lover knows tears and joy, good food and a hungry belly. We are not other than life, because nothing is other.

We are endless and eternal, and our nonexistence is real. And yet at this time and place something is calling the mystic to participate, to take on the clothes of existence and to engage in life. This call does not come from the suffering of the earth or the cries of humanity. The one who has gone beyond life and death is not bound by creation. And yet there is a call, like a note that carries a quality of infinite compassion and an awakening to action. But we must understand that this action *does not belong to the world of cause and effect.*

Between existence and nonexistence, between being and nonbeing, there is a thread that connects the worlds. This thread neither exists nor does not exist. It is and it is not. Because of this quality it has great power and meaning, love and beauty. Mystics know how to work with this thread. They can weave it into existence and yet stay true to its nonexistence. This means that it is essentially free within the patterns of creation. It does not belong to cause and effect, and yet it is also a part of life.

The texture and consistency of this thread is love. It is this thread that is calling mystics to participate more fully in life, because this thread needs to be taken into the arena of action and reaction. It needs to free the drama of life from old patterns that are limiting and constricting. And yet this thread does not belong to life. It belongs to the hidden face of God. This is why it is kept secret. And this is why it needs to be known. The revelation of His secrets is a part of the unfolding pattern of creation. They are the jewels of creation, of His unfolding love. Without them life would slowly become more and more shadowy; its colors would fade, its music die away.

But the revelation of His secrets cannot be sudden or contrived. The amount of light would be blinding. His secrets need to be carefully woven into creation so that His revelation carries the texture of life. This is the work of the mystic, of the one who has passed behind the tapestry of creation and yet returned. And the mystic is being drawn into the dense patterns of matter where this thread needs to be woven. The mystic is not here to save the world; rather she is here for the sake of love's unfolding, which is quite different.

WORKING WHERE EXISTENCE AND NONEXISTENCE MEET

How does one work with what does not exist? How can one be present where one is not? Yet this is the ancient and enduring work of the mystic. From heart to heart, from soul to soul, the ways of the mystic are passed from teacher to disciple. They are also in the book of life, because without the presence of the mystic, life could not unfold. An essential note would be missing. Mystics are taught to read the book of life, to understand its deepest patterns. Because their being is free from surface events, they can read this book and understand its themes. They can learn how to respond to what *is*, rather than being caught in life's reflections. A hidden part of the mystical training is how to respond to the real needs of life, how to work with its substance rather than its appearance.

The substance of life contains life's real meaning and the seeds of its future. The future and the present are not separate, but are variations on a theme. The interrelationship of the future and the present is a subtle process that responds to our attention. But one can only work with the future if one is not attached to its outcome. The future cannot be forced. It is too fluid, too amorphous.

The thread that connects existence and nonexistence is essential to the well-being of the world. Without this thread, existence would become too static, too identified with form. There could be no real change. There could be slight variations but the patterns of life would not evolve. Nonexistence frees existence from stagnation and death. Rumi points to this quality of nonexistence in the simple imagery of the seasons:

In the direction without directions all is spring; any other direction holds nothing but the cold of December.[1]

Present and future evolve together; just as a shoot breaks through the ground, a bud bursts into flower. Mystics work for the future while immersed in the present;

they work with the evolving patterns of life. Because the mystic is not attached to form, she can help life evolve according to a need beyond any concept, any created idea. In Sufism this is imaged by the figure of Khidr, "one whom God had given knowledge of Himself" (Qur'an 18:61). Khidr does not follow any defined path, but acts according to the will of God. His actions are according to the need of the moment, but they also embrace the future.[2]

Because the mystic belongs to both the formless essence and the world of forms, she can work with the continually evolving present in harmony with its source in nonexistence. Where existence and nonexistence meet is where the forms of the future are defined. Here the thread of His love is woven into the patterns of creation, so that when they come into being they reflect His love.

The meeting of existence and nonexistence is a place of great power. Here one can work with a knowledge of sacred names. The cells of creation can be stamped with the name of God. Also, magic can be made on a higher or lower level. One can bring creation in our world into alignment with the movement of the stars, with higher forces in the universe. Or one can use a knowledge of naming or other magic to influence the future, bend creation according to one's will. The patterns of life before they become fixed into form can be subtly shifted, or they can be given a quality of conscious remembrance that brings His presence more visibly into creation.

Where nonexistence and existence come together is the realm of Khidr, who is found "where the two seas meet." He is present in this world, often appearing as an ordinary person. He is rarely recognized, partly because his appearance is so ordinary, but also because he has a quality of nonexistence. Only someone who knows nonexistence can recognize that quality in another.

This simple truth is what hides much mystical work in our world. We cannot see what does not exist. Even the dimension where nonexistence and existence meet is beyond the perception of most people. Only when Khidr has gone do we realize that he has been present. The mystery of presence and absence is a cornerstone of mystical work.[3]

BEYOND THE DUALITY OF BEING AND NONBEING

Existing where being and nonbeing meet, the mystic is immersed in the two worlds. And yet even to think of these different realities as two suggests the illusion of duality. Unity beyond any duality is a primal stamp of mystical truth. The mystic has passed beyond the duality of emptiness and form, nonbeing and being. We know that He hides and reveals Himself. In creation His essential nonbeing is made visible. In essence there is no duality between the phenomenal world and the primordial nothingness. How can there be other than one? Duality is a creation of the mind. The heart knows the deeper truth: that presence and absence are the same. In the emptiness He is present. In form He is present. All is He. And His nature is beyond being and nonbeing:

> Say: He is God the one
> God the self-subsistent, eternally sought
> He begets not nor is He begotten
> And there is nothing to which He can be compared
> (Qur'an 112:1-4).

The mystic subsists in this primal reality, beyond knowing and not-knowing. The freedom from any concept, any identification, enables the mystic to live this oneness. This is what we weave into our life. This is in the imprint of our footsteps; it is the essence of the name we repeat with each and every breath. In the mirror of our heart, polished through our devotion, the light of this primal oneness is reflected. Yet the mirror of our heart is also this oneness. *We* are this oneness.

We make the journey back to God through His longing that is awakened within our heart. We cry His tears, call His name to Him. And when we are united, merged back in the source, His oneness takes on the form of emptiness, of limitless, undefined space. In this space His essential nothingness is revealed and we journey from being to nonbeing. In this journey we realize that there is no journey, that there could never be any separation. There is nothing other than He. His presence and His absence are part of the same essential reality. Emptiness and form are not two.

The lover who is seduced by the Beloved, who is united and merged into love, realizes the oneness beyond duality: "I am He whom I love. He whom I love is me." Creation tells this story again and again; every atom unfolds this drama of love. In the words of the Chan master, Hsu Yun:

> How wide are the horizons of the spinning earth!
> The moonlight leads the tides and the sun's light
>   will not be confined
> Within the net of heaven. But in the end all things
>   return to the One.
> The deaf and the dumb, the crippled and deformed
>   are all restored to One's Perfection.[4]

As we weave the thread of His oneness into life, we help to heal the world of its dualism, of its drama of separation. This work helps a world that has forgotten

Him, "the deaf and the dumb, the crippled and deformed." Because we are immersed in nonbeing, this thread cannot be constricted by form or concept. Because we embrace the world of being, we do not deny His presence. The colors of creation are present, as is the color of nonbeing, "the color of water." Love, laughter, and emptiness—how can we reject anything? We know that every image is His image, and that He has no image.

If we do not limit life with our definitions and expectations, we can help life unfold according to its own way, the way of the primal oneness that is within all of life and of which we are a part. Life needs to return to this oneness, this acceptance of all of its forms as well as a knowing of what is beyond form. Why should life be limited to form? Why should life be constricted by definition? What is really alive cannot be defined, because life belongs to the eternal moment of His creation. Each moment is free and unique; each moment reflects His oneness in a new way. Caught in definition we see life only as an image, not as divine presence. Divine presence by its very nature cannot be defined. It can only be experienced.

The experience of divine presence contains an energy that belongs to emptiness. Creation is a dynamic flowing from emptiness into form and back into emptiness. Each moment is an in-breathing and out-breathing of the creative energy of the divine, in which we knowingly or unknowingly participate:

> In the beginning there was nothing, nor was
>   anything lacking.
> The paper was blank. We pick up the paint brush
>   and create the scene...
> The landscape, the wind whipping water in waves.
> Everything depends upon the stroke of our brush.

> Our Ox lets the good earth lead it,
> Just as our brush allows our hand to move it.
> Take any direction, roam the world to its
>   farthest edge.
> All comes back to where it started...
>   To blessed Emptiness.[5]

If we are too identified with form, we lose the free-dom of emptiness. If we are too lost in emptiness, we forget the wonder of form. The bringing together of form and emptiness allows us to be present and to fully partici-pate in the deeper mystery of creation in which the hidden becomes visible. In this mystery, an aspect of our own divine nature takes on form and yet never loses its essen-tial quality, its primal oneness. As we witness this, we give creation a way to know Him, and thus a way for Him to make Himself known to Himself.

THE INTERPLAY OF FORM AND FORMLESSNESS

A predominant spiritual conditioning suggests it is bet-ter to rest in emptiness than to engage in the play of forms. But any conditioning restricts our real freedom and our capacity to respond to the need of the time. Any concept, any judgment is a denial of what is real. And at this time there is work to be done in the interplay of the formless and the world of forms. Outwardly engaged in form, inwardly immersed in emptiness, "Outwardly to be with the people, inwardly to be with God," we engage in life's ordinary activities while in service to what is Real.

In this interplay of forms and formlessness, a quality of presence is needed that denies neither existence nor nonexistence. We look both to the source and to the flowing river of life that embraces so many forms. In our consciousness these apparent opposites are reconnected, and for the lover this connection is made with love. In the continually changing organic oneness of life something is then redeemed. When we make the connection between form and formlessness, we give life the knowledge of this connection. We free life from the limitation of form and reconnect it with its source in the formless. We help life to remember the root of its own being.

Without emptiness life becomes too constricted, too identified with form. Without form the primordial oneness cannot be reflected into self-knowing. Both emptiness and form have a role to play:

> In the being of a thing,
> There lies the benefit;
> In the non-being of a thing,
> There lies its use.[6]

Human consciousness has the potential to recognize both emptiness and form and to participate in the evolution of divine consciousness, the divine knowing of itself through creation. In the journey of the soul we need to incarnate into the physical world to reach Reality. This is one of the spiritual mysteries of incarnation. The divine comes into physical form in order to know what is Real. What is true for the individual is also true for the planet, for this organic web of life and consciousness we call our world.

On our individual journey we take a significant step when we realize that the phenomenal world is not all that exists. Through meditation and other spiritual disciplines we come to experience a vaster, intangible reality beyond the visible world. As our journey continues, we bring this awareness into our daily life, and the world of illusion becomes a place of revelation. This is when we begin to consciously participate in His knowing of Himself. What happens on an individual level can also happen on a global level. We can participate in the awakening of the world—the world's awareness of itself as a place of revelation.

The work of reconnecting our awareness of the formless with the dimension of forms encounters a collective greed that grasps at forms, that tries to possess the material world. This collective drive channels to itself many of our human and planetary resources, keeping collective attention more and more fixed on form. In previous eras and cultures there was a more fluid interplay between the physical and the invisible world. The physical world was often valued in symbolic terms; outer objects and actions had a symbolic function and meaning. This relationship to the inner symbolic realm nourished the human psyche. But as our Western materialistic culture became more and more dominant, these connections in our collective consciousness were broken, and the physical world became more isolated. Although we may not realize it, this is one of the primary reasons for our global and ecological imbalance. As Carl Jung expressed it, "The world today hangs by a thin thread, and that thread is the psyche of man."[7]

The world needs to be freed from the grasp of materialism and its power drives. One of the ways to do this is to reconnect formlessness and form within the knowing of the heart. Through our hearts, the world can recognize that form has a partner in emptiness and can slip out of the grip of our collective power drives. Without this awareness, the world of forms will become more and more calcified, unable to change or diversify. The world of existence needs our awareness of nonexistence in order to become free. This is a very real contribution that mystics can make to the present global situation.

LIVING IN THE WORLD

Many spiritual texts help the wayfarer journey from the outer to the inner, turn from the world of forms to the formless. These are the roads that have been signposted by those who have gone before us. Less is written about how to return from nonexistence, how to live in the world of forms while staying true to one's essential emptiness. In the Zen Ox-herding pictures, after reaching the source, the sage returns to the world:

> Barefoot and naked of breast, I mingle with the
>   people of the world.
> My clothes are ragged and dust-laden, and I am
>   ever-blissful.
> I use no magic to extend my life;
> Now before me, the dead trees become alive.[8]

And the commentary adds, "I go to the marketplace with my wine bottle and return home with my staff. I visit the wine shop and the market, and everyone I look upon becomes enlightened."[9] But this market seems far from the complexity and clamor of today's marketplace. The forces that we encounter are quite different, as are the demands that life makes on us.

In the emptiness a work can be done that is needed. Knots that are tying the patterns of creation can be freed, a quality of love can flow, a dynamic of joy can return. Through the emptiness something can be given. We know how the emptiness of our own heart is used to give a quality of love and remembrance to another—the strange sweetness as something flows from our essence. A still and empty mind can also be used to reflect a quality of light to another person. The work that is done from heart to heart, from soul to soul, can also be done with the whole world. Through the emptiness of the mystic, something can be given to the world that comes directly from the beyond; an essential substance can be given directly to the heart and consciousness of the world.

The mystic is an empty doorway to the beyond. Most energy that comes into the world comes down through the planes of manifestation. Each plane is slightly denser and more veiled, and so the pure light is distorted. Through the mystic a quality of light can flow almost undistorted. The heart and mind of the mystic have been trained to do this work, to reflect light and love in such a way that this energy is distorted as little as possible. This is one of the reasons that mystics need to have a certain purity, focused intention, and nonattachment to form. (Of course the mystic also needs to be unattached to any spiritual ideal or image of purity.) The mystic is like a lens that can direct the light from nonbeing into being. If a lens is not polished, the light will be distorted.

The density and demands of today's marketplace, filled with materialistic thoughts and soul-denying corporate pressures, create a particular challenge for someone who has been immersed in emptiness. It is no longer appropriate to renounce the world, and yet it is so easy to get caught in the images and illusions that bombard us. The simplicity of the Zen sage in the market seems unrealistic. The essence of life may remain simple, but its colors have become complex. Life has to show us a new way to be, a new way to walk in which emptiness and form come together. Life is always full of limitations; everyday demands are a necessary part of its play. But if we let life relate to us, it can open in unexpected ways. For this to happen we first have to acknowledge that life is alive and belongs to God. Then we allow life its full potential to change.

Emptiness and form are partners in life. The womb is an empty space waiting to give birth to new forms. Even the simple wonder of making love is a meeting of form and emptiness, masculine and feminine. If we learn how to make love to life, then life can give birth. Each time we impose ourself upon life, it is a violation. Sadly many of our ideas about saving the world are an imposition, not born from a real relationship with our planet. We have forgotten how to speak to life and how to listen. We do not know how to create a space when we ask a question. One of the most valuable models psychotherapy provides is of a place of listening and being heard. Life has a deep need to be heard. If we listen, we may discover that what we have diagnosed as problems are just miscommunications or misunderstandings.

It is a deep spiritual truth that everything is just the way it should be. This truth is not a denial of life's challenges, but an awareness of a deeper level of being. If we approach life in this way, we may find that life changes in unexpected ways. We are unaware of the real dynamics of our interaction with life, how our patterns of relationship affect life. Psychotherapy has shown us how personal and family relationships are constellated by our attitudes, and how a simple shift in attitude can dramatically change both ourself and those around us. Patterns of action and reaction that had seemed fixed start to flow and problems that appeared irresolvable can be reconciled or fall away. We can bring this understanding into our relationship with all of life. If we recognize that life is an organic whole, a vast family of interrelationships, we can learn how to listen, and to see how our attitude can help these interrelationships shift into more beneficial patterns.

The mystic can bring her experience of emptiness and formlessness into her relationship with life. In our individual journey, the experience of nonbeing is very liberating. The patterns of the ego fall away when confronted by our nonexistence. The same can be true in our relationship to life. We can help to free life of some of the constricted patterns our patriarchal past has imposed upon it. Through the relationship between the core of our being and the core of life, a different energy can flow. The organic web of life will respond to this energy in ways we cannot imagine. Certain new forms can be born only in emptiness. The emptiness of the mystic has a quality of primordial awareness that is a catalyst for things coming together in new ways, for new forms being born. The presence of this quality in the world works like the presence of Khidr, who removes obstacles and brings the unexpected into being.

The sage who lives his essential emptiness makes "dead trees come alive." In the story told in the Qur'an, Khidr is found where the two seas meet, and where the "dead fish comes alive." The Buddhist sage and Khidr image a simple reality of life that has a transformative effect. The mystic is one who has access to this quality of being that belongs to our primordial nature. It cannot be caught in any form, in any defined pattern. And it brings to life what had appeared dead.

In our daily life we walk the pathless path of the mystic, uniting being and nonbeing, form and formlessness. We allow life to change around us, opening a space for the unexpected to happen. Through our empty presence a certain frequency of energy can come into the world. Through our essential nonbeing, grace can be given freely.

This transmission of energy or grace that can only come from the beyond is needed for the transformation of life. It is needed for a new way of relating to life to be reflected into consciousness. In our individual journey we need this energy that is given freely in order to make a certain step. We cannot make this step on our own. The same is true of the evolution of the world. Through the union of emptiness and form something can be given. Only then will the heart of the world awaken and sing, and all life reflect a new expression of the infinite.

APPENDIX:
THE ARCHETYPE
of the NEW AGE

The emerging archetype can be seen as the number eight, the number of infinity, which is also the number of the union of the inner and outer worlds. The number eight images the flow of energy between the infinite and the finite, the inner and outer.

The great archetypal beings, the kings and queens of the inner world, are numbered seven. Astrology, the science of the psyche, saw them as the seven major planetary bodies: the sun, the moon, Saturn, Jupiter, Mercury, Venus, and Mars. The outer planets, Uranus, Neptune, and Pluto, have only been discovered in the last two hundred years, but for the last three or four thousand years seven has been the number of the inner and outer cosmos. There were the seven great Babylonian gods, which in the *Book of Enoch* became the seven Archons, rulers of "this world."[1] In the *Book of Zechariah* there are the seven eyes of God on the cornerstone for the new temple, which suggests the seven stars, "the planetary gods who were depicted by the alchemists in a cave under the earth"; they are the seven sleepers "enchained in Hades."[2] In the *Book of Revelation* there are the seven stars in the right hand of the Son of Man.[3] Shakespeare's famous speech "Seven Ages of Man" in *As You Like It* reflects the planetary periods of life. This sevenfold division of the cosmos suggests that there are seven major archetypal energies or types of energy, which are even imaged in the days of the week.

But the gods have not always been numbered seven. At one time there were six great deities. Then, between three and four thousand years ago, Zoroaster realized that these six deities were aspects of the One Great God. In counting the six deities he added the seventh number, which was all the six together. This is a method of counting which later spread to India and Tibet, in which you count the objects and then add one for their totality. The number seven formed of the One Great God with six attributes can be seen in the biblical numbering of the days of creation. There are the six days of His actual creation, and one day for Himself alone, on which He rested.

We no longer project the seven great archetypes onto the planets. We have rediscovered them within the psyche. They are aspects of our own deepest nature, contained within the wholeness of the Self. As we individually relate to these primal powers, we *consciously* accept them as a part of ourself. This is the process of conscious awareness and responsibility that forms the new emerging archetype: the seven contained within the one form an eighth. It can be imaged as the child of the new age, who is our own essential nature; in it the name and purpose of each living thing is known. In its new-born wholeness it knows everything; nothing is excluded. In the eyes of this child each atom of creation has its place in the unfolding music of life. The child is a living symbol of harmony and wholeness, and like the seven archetypes, it is a part of us. The song of the child sings in our blood.

This child is the emerging archetype, the symbol of the coming age. Yet unlike the other archetypes, the essence of the child is a space rather than a form, a sacred space in which we can be our true selves and experience the joy which belongs to life itself. This space can also be seen as "a stage" which I saw in a vision:

> Slowly a curtain rises on a new stage. Your own life is this stage. Yet even the idea of a stage is a limitation because it belongs to the world of forms. The stage of the future is not a structure. It is a quality of closeness, a quality of intimacy, a quality of touching and of allowing yourself to be touched. It is a quality of sharing something most secret always, of being shown something most secret always. It is a quality of togetherness, of being together with yourself, of becoming familiar with yourself, of not forcing yourself into corners or pushing yourself back against a wall. It has to do with freeing yourself of so many restrictions that are totally irrelevant, for they belong to another time.

The deepest meaning of the inner world can only unfold into our life when we are true to ourself, when we live our own life, singing our own song. We each have our own destiny, our own unique way of living what is most precious. For some it can be baking bread with love, for others, painting a picture. Jung says, "Find the meaning and make the meaning your goal." The archetype of the future holds a sacred space, a temple without walls in which everything is holy, in which this deep meaning can be lived, the sacred moment be now. In this moment we are open to life, to the miracle of being human and the wonder of being divine.

The child of the future is a space that gives us the inner freedom and power to catch the thread of our story and weave it into our life. Then we can feel the oneness

that belongs to the Self, hidden within the surface multiplicity. We know ourself to be a part of this oneness,
and our own life to belong to the mystery of the word
Kun! [Be].

*N*OTES

INTRODUCTION

1. "The World," *The Works of Henry Vaughan*, ed. L. C. Martin.
2. *The Thirteen Principle Upanishads*, trans. R. E. Hume.
3. Llewellyn Vaughan-Lee, *The Bond with the Beloved*, pp. 37–38.
4. See Vaughan-Lee, *Working with Oneness*.

1. LIGHT OF ONENESS

1. *Mandaka Upanishad* 2.2.10–11, *The Upanishads*, trans. Eknath Easwaran.
2. *The Secret of Secrets*, trans. Tosun Bayrak, p. xlvii.
3. In astrology the past age was symbolized by the two fishes, and the split between matter and spirit was emphasized.
4. C. G. Jung, *Psychological Reflections*, p. 39.

2. AWAKENING THE WORLD

1. "Searching for the Dharma," by Hsu Yun.
2. Nizami, *The Story of Layla and Majnun*, trans. R. Gelpke, p. 195.
3. Quoted by Al-Hassan Abdel-Kader, *The Life, Personality and Writings of Al-Junayd*, p. 90.
4. Quoted by Abdel-Kader, p. 90. For a fuller commentary on this state of *fanâ*, see Vaughan-Lee, *The Circle of Love*, pp. 141–146.
5. Ibn 'Arabî, trans. William Chittick, *The Sufi Path of Knowledge*, p. 364.

3. LIFE'S INTERCONNECTION

1. *The Gift*, trans. Daniel Ladinsky, p. 265.
2. Wing-tsit Chan, comp. and trans., *A Source Book in Chinese Philosophy*, Doctrine of the Mean, 22.
3. Tulku Urgyen Rinpoche, *Repeating the Words of the Buddha*, p. 60.
4. "Saving the Indigenous Soul," *The Sun*, April 2001, Issue 304.
5. Holy Bible (Revised Standard Edition), *Hosea* 4:1–3.

4. REFLECTIONS OF LIGHT

1. Ibn 'Arabî describes this dimension, where things reveal their essence through their light: "When I entered into this waystation, the self-disclosure without rays fell upon me, so I saw it knowingly. I saw myself through it and I saw all things through myself and through the lights which things carry in their essences and which are given to them by their realities, not through any extraneous light." Quoted in William Chittick, *The Sufi Path of Knowledge*, p. 218.
2. In the Sufi tradition Najm al-dîn Kubrâ (d. 1220) is one of the masters who write about light. See Henry Corbin, *The Man of Light in Iranian Sufism*.
3. Ibn 'Arabî, quoted by Chittick, p. 215.
4. Irina Tweedie, *Daughter of Fire*, p. 523.
5. See Appendix.

5. POWERS OF DARKNESS

1. Corbin describes this as the "luminous night of *superconsciousness*, the Divine darkness, the cloud of unknowing" (*The Man of Light*, p. 7). He refers to the mystical recitals of Avicenna which describe this as "the darkness at the approaches to the *pole*" in contrast to "the darkness reigning at the 'Far West' of matter. The latter is the darkness whose behavior in regard to light is described by physics; these are the forces of darkness that retain the light, obstruct its passage ... called by the ancient Iranian term of *barzakh* (screen, barrier)." Corbin, *The Man of Light*, p. 101.
2. Ibn 'Arabî, quoted by Chittick, *The Sufi Path of Knowledge*, p. 196.
3. I have written about this extensively in *The Signs of God*, especially pp. 93–105.
4. Quoted by Timothy Freke and Peter Gandy, *Jesus and the Lost Goddess*, p. 169.
5. The Gnostics also associated the Demiurge with evil. See C. G. Jung, *Collected Works*, vol. 9ii, para. 233. In Sufi symbolism light belongs to the heavenly pole, the mystic orient, while darkness reigns at the far west of matter. (See the recitals of Avicenna, Corbin, p. 101.)
6. C. G. Jung, *Collected Works*, vol. 11, para. 92.

6. FREEDOM

1. Trans. R. H. Blyth, *Zen in English Literature and Oriental Classics*, p. 298.
2. Kees W. Bolle, ed., *The Bhagavadgita: A New Translation*, 5.24.
3. *The Gift*, trans. Daniel Ladinsky, p. 28.

7. PEACE

1. Quoted by A. Devaraja Mudaliar, *Day by Day with Bhagavan*, p. 15.
2. Irina Tweedie, *Daughter of Fire*, p. 404.
3. Holy Bible (Authorized Version), St. John, 14:27.
4. *Midrash*, Exodus Rabbah (31:15), trans. H. Freedman and Maurice Simon.

8. THE ENERGY OF MATTER

1. *The Book of Secrets*, trans. from the French by Lynn Finegan.
2. William Chittick, *The Sufi Path of Knowledge*, pp. 154–5.
3. *Tao Te Ching*, trans. Gia-Fu Feng and Jane English, Fifty-Nine.
4. Heisenberg's Uncertainty Principle, "The more precisely the position is known, the less precisely the momentum is known," points to this dynamic.
5. See Llewellyn Vaughan-Lee, *Working with Oneness*, ch. 7, "Magic."
6. Martin Prechtel, "Saving the Indigenous Soul," *The Sun*, April 2001.
7. Rumi, trans. Andrew Harvey, *The Mystic Vision*, p. 144.
8. Shabistari, *The Secret Rose Garden*, trans. Florence Lederer, p. 85.

9. NONBEING AND BEING

1. *The Sufi Path of Love*, William Chittick, p. 23.
2. This is evident in the story of Moses and Khidr told in the Qur'an (*sura* 18:61–83). Khidr's first action was to bore a hole in the ship in which they were traveling, because, as Khidr explained, "The ship belonged to some poor fishermen. I damaged it because if it had gone to sea it would have been captured by a king who was seizing every boat by force."
3. "He is where he is not and he is not where he is." Al-Junayd. See above p. 42.
4. Master Hsu Yun, *Poems on the Oxherding Series*.
5. Ibid.

6. *Tao Te Ching, A New Translation with Commentary*, Ellen M. Chen.

7. *Psychological Reflections*, p. 14.

8. *Zen Flesh, Zen Bones*, ed. Paul Reps, p. 186.

9. Ibid.

APPENDIX: THE ARCHETYPE OF THE NEW AGE

1. C. G. Jung, *Collected Works*, 12, para. 298.

2. C. G. Jung, *Collected Works*, 9i, para. 246n.

3. Holy Bible (King James Version), *Revelation of St. John the Divine*, 1:16.

ℬIBLIOGRAPHY

Abdel-Kader, Al- Hassan. *The Life, Personality and Writings of Al-Junayd*. London: Luzac & Company, 1976.

Al-Jîlânî. *The Secret of Secrets*. Trans. Tosun Bayrak. Cambridge: Islamic Texts Society, 1992.

Attâr, Farîd ud-Dîn. *The Book of Secrets*. Trans. Lynn Finegan. Unpublished.

Blyth, R. H. *Zen in English Literature and Oriental Classics*. Tokyo: The Hokuseido Press, 1942.

Bolle, Kees W., ed. *The Bhagavadgita: A New Translation*. Berkeley: University of California Press, 1979.

Chittick, William. *The Sufi Path of Love*. Albany: State University of New York Press, 1983.

—. *The Sufi Path of Knowledge*. Albany: State University of New York Press, 1989.

Corbin, Henry. *The Man of Light in Iranian Sufism*. London: Shambhala, 1978.

Easwaran, Eknath, trans. *The Upanishads*. Petaluma, California: Nilgiri Press, 1985.

Freedman, H. and Maurice Simon, trans. *Midrash*. New York: Soncino Press, 1983.

Freke, Timothy and Peter Gandy. *Jesus and the Lost Goddess*. New York: Random House, 2001.

Hafiz. *The Gift*. Trans. Daniel Ladinsky. New York: Arkana, Penguin Group, 1999.

Harvey, Andrew and Anne Baring. *The Mystic Vision*. Alresford: Godsfield Press, 1995.

Holy Bible, Authorized Version.

Holy Bible, King James Version.

Holy Bible, Revised Standard Edition.

Hsu Yun. *Six Poems by Hsu Yun*. www.hsuyun.org.

—. *Poems on the Oxherding Series*. www.hsuyun.org

Hume, R. E., trans. *The Thirteen Principle Upanishads*. Oxford: Oxford University Press, 1931.

Jung, C. G. *Collected Works*. London: Routledge & Kegan Paul.

—. *Psychological Reflections*. London: Routledge & Kegan Paul, 1953.

Lao Tsu. *Tao Te Ching*. Trans. Gia-Fu Feng and Jane English. Aldershot: Wildwood House Ltd., 1973.

—. *Tao Te Ching, A New Translation with Commentary*. Trans. and ed. Ellen M. Chen. New York: Paragon House, 1989.

Nizami. *The Story of Layla and Majnun*. Trans. R. Gelpke. London: Bruno Cassirer, 1966.

Mudaliar, A. Devaraja. *Day by Day with Bhagavan*. Sri Ramana Maharshi, 1977.

Reps, Paul, ed. *Zen Flesh, Zen Bones*. Boston: Tuttle Publishing, 1957.

Shabistari. *The Secret Rose Garden*. Trans. Florence Lederer. Grand Rapids, Michigan: Phanes Press, 1987.

Tulku Urgyen Rinpoche. *Repeating the Words of the Buddha*. Kathmandu: Rangjung Yeshe Publications, 1992.

Tweedie, Irina. *Daughter of Fire: A Diary of a Spiritual Training with a Sufi Master*. Nevada City: Blue Dolphin Publishing, 1986.

Vaughan, Henry. *The Works of Henry Vaughan*. Ed. L. C. Martin. Oxford: Oxford University Press, 1914.

Vaughan-Lee, Llewellyn. *The Bond with the Beloved*. Inverness, California: The Golden Sufi Center, 1993.

—. *The Circle of Love*. Inverness, California: The Golden Sufi Center, 1999.

—. *The Signs of God*. Inverness, California: The Golden Sufi Center, 2001.

—. *Working with Oneness*. Inverness, California: The Golden Sufi Center, 2002.

Wing-tsit Chan, comp. and trans. *A Source Book in Chinese Philosophy*. Princeton: Princeton University Press, 1963.

ᴊNDEX

A

Abu Sa'id ibn Abî-l-Khayr (d. 1049) 65
alchemist 55, 108, 174
anima mundi xxi, 108
annihilation 41, 42
archetype, archetypal 33, 34, 56, 84, 96, 130, 136, 174-176
Attâr, Farîduddîn, (d. 1220) 138
attention xiv, 24, 31, 39, 51-54, 60-64, 69, 76, 85, 91, 96, 97, 98, 106, 113, 127, 158, 161, 168
Avicenna (d. 1037) 179
awakened heart 25, 51
awe 11
awliyâ (see also friends of God) xix, 65

B

baqâ 42
Bhagavad Gita 111
Bhai Sahib (d. 1966) 81, 125
bodhisattva 49, 65
book of life 161
Book of Revelation 174
breath 38, 42, 43, 50, 54, 133, 136, 164
Buddha 158, 178
Buddhism, Buddhist 27, 38, 49, 60, 61, 65, 172

C

centers of power 33, 34
chain of love 26
Chartres Cathedral 80
Christ 125, 126, 128
Christian, Christianity 107, 115
collective consciousness xvi, 32, 33, 65, 82, 86, 90, 91, 106, 119, 127, 128, 168
collective forgetfulness 29
collective psyche xiv, xvi, 96, 98, 136, 137
collective thought-forms 32, 86, 113, 115
compassion xviii, 38, 49, 60, 64, 95, 98, 159
Confucian 58
consciousness of love 49, 54, 55, 61, 64, 66
of oneness xiii, xiii, 25, 28, 31, 46, 49, 50, 54, 98
global consciousness 83, 116, 119
constellation of opposites xiv, 132
Corbin, Henry (d. 1978) 179

D

demiurge 107, 108, 179
deus absconditus 93
devil 107
dharma 36, 49
dhikr 38, 103
divine presence xiv, 62, 165

ABOUT *the* AUTHOR

LLEWELLYN VAUGHAN-LEE, Ph.D., is a Sufi Teacher in the Naqshbandiyya-Mujaddidiyya Sufi Order. Born in London in 1953, he has followed the Naqshbandi Sufi path since he was 19. In 1991 he moved to Northern California and became the successor of Irina Tweedie, author of *Chasm of Fire* and *Daughter of Fire*. In recent years the focus of his writing and teaching has been on spiritual responsibility in our present time of transition, and the emerging global consciousness of oneness. He has also specialized in the area of dreamwork, integrating the ancient Sufi approach to dreams with the insights of modern psychology. Author of several books, Llewellyn lectures throughout the United States and Europe.

ABOUT *the* PUBLISHER

THE GOLDEN SUFI CENTER is a California Religious Non-Profit Corporation dedicated to making the teachings of the Naqshbandi Sufi path available to all seekers. For further information about the activities and publications, please contact:

THE GOLDEN SUFI CENTER
P.O. Box 428
Inverness, CA 94937-0428
tel: 415-663-8773 · *fax:* 415-663-9128
info@goldensufi.org · www.goldensufi.org

ADDITIONAL PUBLICATIONS
from THE GOLDEN SUFI CENTER

by IRINA TWEEDIE

DAUGHTER OF FIRE:
A Diary of a Spiritual Training with a Sufi Master

by LLEWELLYN VAUGHAN-LEE

WORKING WITH ONENESS

THE SIGNS OF GOD

LOVE IS A FIRE:
The Sufi's Mystical Journey Home

THE CIRCLE OF LOVE

CATCHING THE THREAD:
Sufism, Dreamwork, and Jungian Psychology

THE FACE BEFORE I WAS BORN:
A Spiritual Autobiography

THE PARADOXES OF LOVE

SUFISM, THE TRANSFORMATION OF THE HEART

IN THE COMPANY OF FRIENDS:
Dreamwork within a Sufi Group

THE BOND WITH THE BELOVED:
The Mystical Relationship of the Lover and the Beloved

edited *by* LLEWELLYN VAUGHAN-LEE
with biographical information by SARA SVIRI

TRAVELLING THE PATH OF LOVE:
Sayings of Sufi Masters

by PETER KINGSLEY

REALITY

IN THE DARK PLACES OF WISDOM

by SARA SVIRI

THE TASTE OF HIDDEN THINGS:
Images of the Sufi Path

by HILARY HART

THE UNKNOWN SHE:
Eight Faces of an Emerging Consciousness